INDIA
in Pictures

VGS

Lee Engfer

Lerner Publications Company

Contents

Lerner Publishing Group realizes that current information and statistics quickly become out of date. To extend the usefulness of the Visual Geography Series, we developed www.vgsbooks.com, a website offering links to up-to-date information, as well as in-depth material, on a wide variety of subjects. All of the websites listed on www.vgsbooks.com have been carefully selected by researchers at Lerner Publishing Group. However, Lerner Publishing Group is not responsible for the accuracy or suitability of the material on any website other than <www.lernerbooks.com>. It is recommended that students using the Internet be supervised by a parent or teacher. Links on www.vgsbooks.com will be regularly reviewed and updated as needed.

Website address: www.lernerbooks.com

Lerner Publications Company
A division of Lerner Publishing Group
241 First Avenue North
Minneapolis, MN 55401 U.S.A.

web enhanced @ www.vgsbooks.com

Library of Congress Cataloging-in-Publication Data

Engfer, Lee, 1963-
India in pictures / by Lee Engfer—Rev. & expanded.
p. cm. — (Visual geography series)
Summary: Text and illustrations present detailed information on the geography, history and government, economy, people, cultural life and society of traditional and modern India.
Includes bibliographical references and index.
ISBN: 0-8225-0371-9 (lib. bdg. : alk. paper)
1. India—Juvenile literature. [1. India.] I. Title. II. Visual geography series (Minneapolis, Minn.)
DS407 .E53 2003
954—dc21 2002000950

Manufactured in the United States of America
1 2 3 4 5 6 - JR - 08 07 06 05 04 03

INTRODUCTION

India is a land of amazing diversity and fabulous contrasts. With an ancient civilization and the second largest population in the world, India is a multilingual, multireligious, multiethnic, and multipolitical nation. It spans the old and the modern, balancing high technology and traditional handicrafts, wealth and poverty, and a creed of nonviolence against ongoing conflicts.

India's population exceeded 1 billion people in 2000 and has since risen to almost 1.3 billion, making it the second most populous country in the world after China. Although almost 350 million Indians live in cities, most of the population lives in rural areas. Indians come from several different ethnic backgrounds and speak hundreds of languages. Religion shapes many aspects of life in India, from food to politics. The majority of the population is Hindu, but followers of Islam, Sikhism, Christianity, Buddhism, and Jainism also make up the nation's citizenry.

After a series of economic reforms in the early 1990s, India showed impressive economic growth during the late 1990s and early 2000s.

The country has one of the fastest-growing economies in Asia and has emerged as a software superpower. Agriculture remains the anchor of the economy, and much of the population depends on farming to earn a living.

Many of the most difficult issues the country faces stem from its burgeoning population. If current trends continue, India will have the world's largest population by 2045. Overpopulation strains the country's resources and harms the environment. Delhi, Mumbai (formerly Bombay), and Chennai are among the world's most polluted cities, and many Indians lack access to clean drinking water and sewer services.

India has launched satellites to orbit the earth, sent an astronaut into space, and developed nuclear weapons. At the same time, however, almost one-third of India's population—and half its women—cannot read or write. The ancient caste system, which divides people into different social groups, continues to play a role in Indian society, although discrimination by caste is officially illegal.

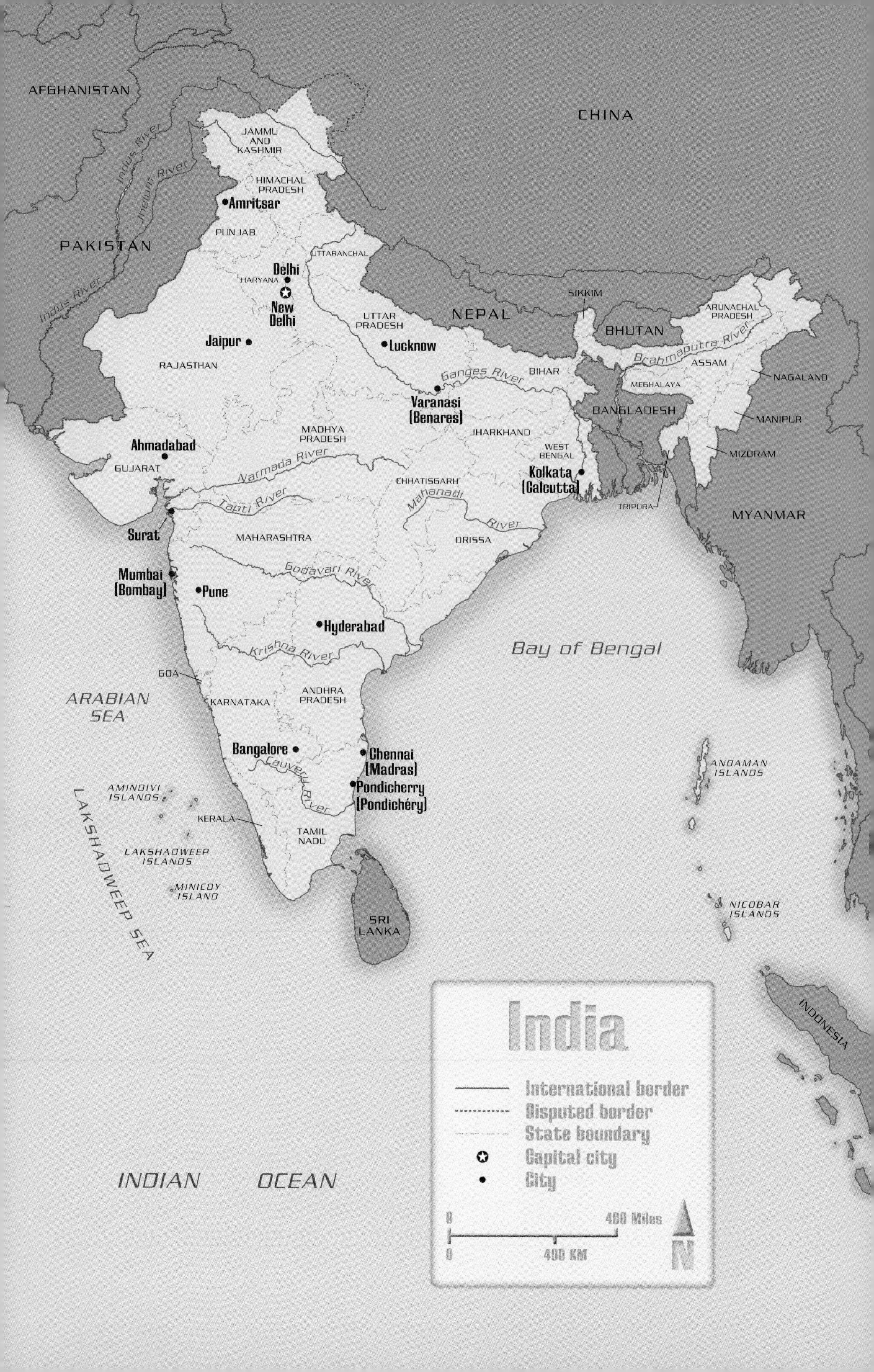

AFGHANISTAN
CHINA
PAKISTAN
JAMMU AND KASHMIR
HIMACHAL PRADESH
Amritsar
PUNJAB
UTTARANCHAL
Delhi
HARYANA
New Delhi
Indus River
Jhelum River
NEPAL
SIKKIM
BHUTAN
ARUNACHAL PRADESH
UTTAR PRADESH
Lucknow
Jaipur
RAJASTHAN
Brahmaputra River
ASSAM
NAGALAND
Ganges River
BIHAR
MEGHALAYA
Varanasi (Benares)
BANGLADESH
MANIPUR
MADHYA PRADESH
JHARKHAND
WEST BENGAL
MIZORAM
Ahmadabad
GUJARAT
Narmada River
Kolkata (Calcutta)
CHHATISGARH
Mahanadi River
TRIPURA
MYANMAR
Tapti River
Surat
MAHARASHTRA
ORISSA
Godavari River
Mumbai (Bombay)
Pune
Hyderabad
Bay of Bengal
Krishna River
GOA
ARABIAN SEA
KARNATAKA
ANDHRA PRADESH
Bangalore
Chennai (Madras)
Cauvery River
Pondicherry (Pondichéry)
ANDAMAN ISLANDS
AMINDIVI ISLANDS
KERALA
TAMIL NADU
LAKSHADWEEP ISLANDS
LAKSHADWEEP SEA
MINICOY ISLAND
NICOBAR ISLANDS
SRI LANKA
INDONESIA
India
International border
Disputed border
State boundary
Capital city
City
0
400 Miles
0
400 KM
N
INDIAN OCEAN

While the middle class in India is growing, so is the divide between middle-class families and the large number of people living in poverty. Although India produces enough food to feed the nation, many children go hungry because their families do not earn enough money to buy food.

Another challenge for India is its ongoing conflict with neighboring Pakistan. Pakistan was part of India until 1947, when India gained independence from Great Britain and was divided along religious lines into two separate countries. Since then, India and Pakistan have fought over disputed territory in the Kashmir region, at the northwestern edge of India. Both countries carried out controversial nuclear test explosions in 1998. Government leaders from India and Pakistan have tried to resolve the conflict, but the dispute remains explosive.

India's relationship with the United States became critical after September 11, 2001, when Islamic terrorists attacked the World Trade Center and the Pentagon in the United States, killing thousands of people. The United States went to war against the Taliban rulers of Afghanistan, Pakistan's neighbor to the north, accusing the government of harboring the terrorist leaders behind the September 11 attacks. The United States became more involved in the region than it had been in decades as it sought the cooperation of both India and Pakistan in the campaign against terrorism. To meet that goal, the United States worked to hold down tensions between the two nuclear rivals.

In the twenty-first century, Indians have cause for both hope and concern. While poverty remains widespread and overpopulation and environmental problems threaten the nation's health, gradual progress is taking place on many fronts. Drawing on its political and economic strengths, India will continue to look for ways to harness its enormous potential.

A blend of the past and the present, **Delhi** captures the contrasts and diversity of India. The India Gate is one of the city's famous sites.

THE LAND

India's varied landscape encompasses some of the tallest mountains in the world, as well as vast deserts, tropical forests, fertile plains, sacred rivers, coastline along three seas, and huge cities. With a large array of wildlife and plants, India is one of twelve "megadiversity" countries, which together account for 70 percent of the world's biodiversity.

Most of India is a peninsula surrounded by three large bodies of water—the Arabian Sea to the west, the Indian Ocean to the south, and the Bay of Bengal to the east. India is bounded on the northwest and north by Pakistan, China, Nepal, and Bhutan, and on the east by Myanmar. Bangladesh cuts between the eastern Indian states of West Bengal, Meghalaya, and Assam. The island nation of Sri Lanka lies 40 miles (64.4 kilometers) southeast of India in the Bay of Bengal.

India is the seventh largest country in the world, covering about 1.3 million square miles (3.3 million square kilometers). Its area equals a little more than one-third of the continental United States. Included in India's national territory are several small islands.

Major Landforms

India's varied terrain is made up of three main regions. In the extreme north are the Himalaya Mountains. South of the Himalayas and their foothills lies the vast, mostly flat Indo-Gangetic Plain, which extends into Pakistan, Nepal, and Bangladesh. In southern, or peninsular, India, the Deccan Plateau is surrounded by three low mountain ranges.

Millions of years ago, two sections of a huge landmass called Gondwanaland collided, creating the Himalaya Mountains. The tallest mountain range in the world, the Himalayas separate India from the rest of Asia. The entire range extends for 1,500 miles (2,400 km) in an arc from northern to northeastern India. The Himalayas contain India's highest mountain, Kanchenjunga (28,146 feet/8,598 meters), which lies on the border with Nepal.

The Indo-Gangetic Plain is named for the two great rivers—the Indus and the Ganges—that border it on the west and east. Most of this 200-mile-wide (322-km) plain consists of flat, well-watered land.

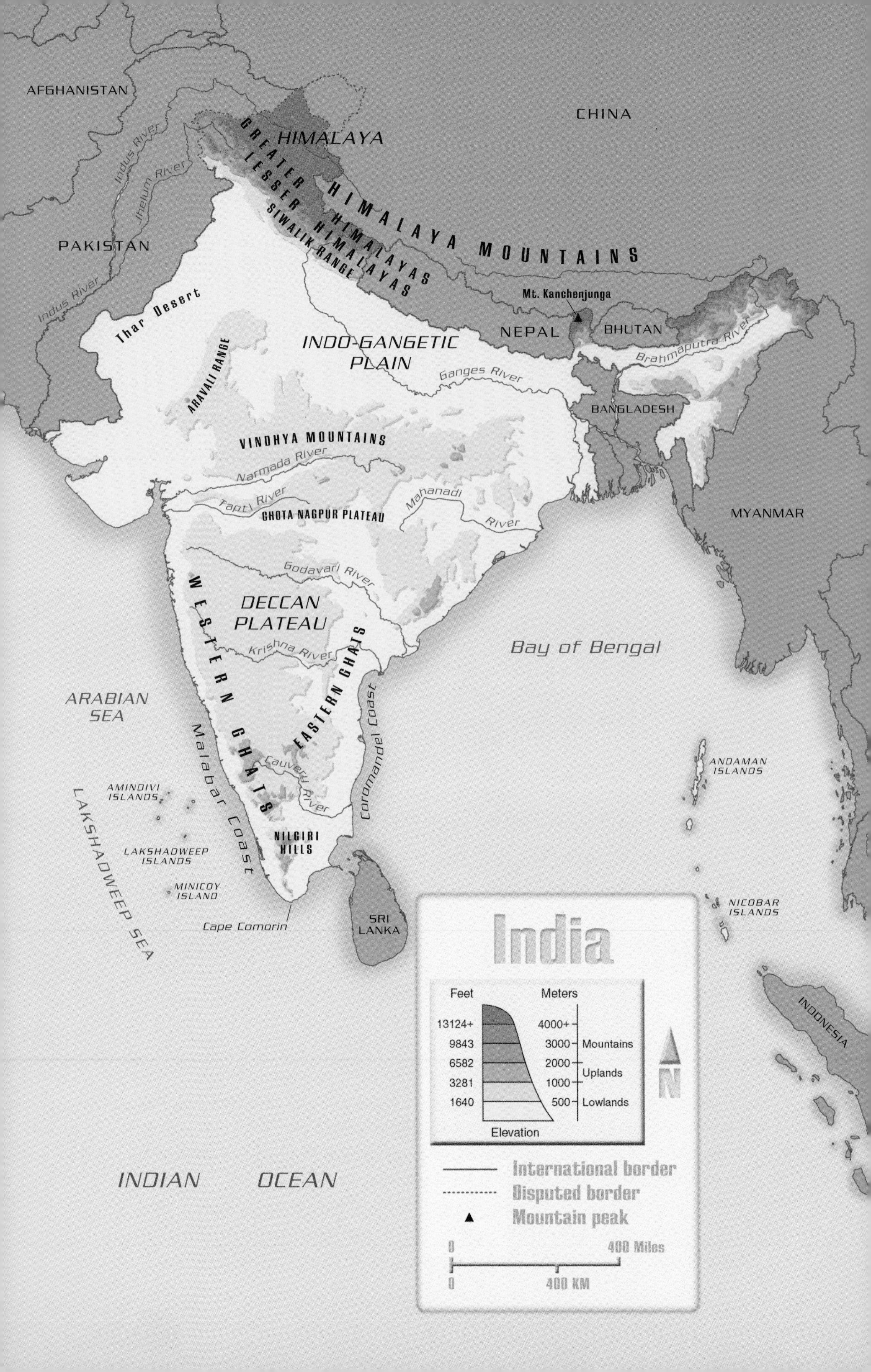

AFGHANISTAN
CHINA
HIMALAYA
GREATER HIMALAYA MOUNTAINS
LESSER HIMALAYAS
SIWALIK RANGE
HIMALAYAS
PAKISTAN
Indus River
Jhelum River
Thar Desert
Mt. Kanchenjunga
NEPAL
BHUTAN
INDO-GANGETIC PLAIN
Brahmaputra River
Ganges River
ARAVALLI RANGE
BANGLADESH
VINDHYA MOUNTAINS
Narmada River
Tapti River
Mahanadi River
CHOTA NAGPUR PLATEAU
MYANMAR
Godavari River
WESTERN GHATS
DECCAN PLATEAU
Krishna River
EASTERN GHATS
Bay of Bengal
ARABIAN SEA
Malabar Coast
Coromandel Coast
Cauvery River
ANDAMAN ISLANDS
AMINDIVI ISLANDS
LAKSHADWEEP SEA
LAKSHADWEEP ISLANDS
NILGIRI HILLS
MINICOY ISLAND
NICOBAR ISLANDS
Cape Comorin
SRI LANKA
India
Feet
Meters
13124+
9843
6582
3281
1640
4000+
3000
2000
1000
500
Mountains
Uplands
Lowlands
Elevation
N
INDONESIA
INDIAN OCEAN
International border
Disputed border
Mountain peak
0
400 Miles
0
400 KM

Since its formation millions of years ago, the northern plain has collected thousands of tons of fertile earth. During and after the monsoons—seasonal winds that bring heavy rains—rivers roar down the steep mountain gorges, eroding rock along the way and carrying silt and minerals to the plain.

Thar Desert

The western section of the Indo-Gangetic Plain is much drier. It merges into the Thar Desert in the states of Rajasthan and Gujarat. The Indo-Gangetic Plain lies along the geologically unstable meeting point of two sections of the earth's crust. As a result, the region is prone to earthquakes.

Southern India, made up mostly of the Deccan Plateau, is a single plate of land. As a result, the Deccan Plateau has been geologically stable for a long time, unlike the Himalayas and the Indo-Gangetic Plain, which were formed from continental movement in more recent geological time.

The triangle-shaped Deccan Plateau begins south of the Narmada River and comes to a point in the southern state of Tamil Nadu. Averaging between 1,000 and 2,300 feet (300 to 700 m) above sea level, the plateau includes rolling hills and many rivers. Surrounding the Deccan Plateau on three sides are low mountain ranges. To the north, the Vindhya Mountains, reaching a peak of 3,651 feet (1,107 m), separate the plateau from the Indo-Gangetic Plain.

"India is the sum of a million worlds enclosed by oceans on three sides, by the mighty Himalayas on the north. Within these boundaries are voluptuous eastern cultures circled by rice fields and western desert kingdoms locked in stone fortifications. Descendants of India's earliest inhabitants occupy the jungles sweeping through her heartland: three-thousand-year-old sacred cities still flourish on the banks of her immense rivers; merchant cultures still grow rich from her ancient ports."

—Gita Mehta, *Snakes and Ladders*

A coastal strip separates the Eastern Ghats from the Bay of Bengal. This 500-mile-long (800-km) mountain range averages 1,500 to 2,000 feet (450 to 600 m) in height. Another coastal belt divides the Western Ghats from the Arabian Sea. These mountains stretch for 800 miles (1,288 km) along the western coast and reach heights of 3,000 to 5,000 feet (900 to 1,500 m). The two ranges merge in southern India at the Nilgiri Hills in Tamil Nadu.

Rivers

India has several long rivers, flanked by stretches of fertile soil. Northern waterways are fed by the melting snows of the Himalayas. The principal waterways in northern India are the Ganges, with its many tributaries; the Indus; and the Brahmaputra.

The 1,500-mile-long (2,400-km) Ganges, called the Ganga in India, is India's greatest river. From the Himalayas, it flows south into the Indo-Gangetic Plain. Eventually, the river travels east to join the Brahmaputra River, and together they empty into the Bay of Bengal at Kolkata (Calcutta). Because of agricultural runoff, industrial waste, and contamination from sewage, the Ganges is one of the most polluted rivers in India. Nonetheless, it is still important for agricultural irrigation. Hindus regard "Ganga Mai" (Mother Ganges) as sacred, and thousands of people drink and bathe in its waters.

The Indus River originates in southern China and flows mostly through Pakistan. A small section of the river also lies within Jammu and Kashmir, a territory claimed by both India and Pakistan.

The **Ganges River** (Ganga Mai, or Mother Ganges) is sacred to Hindus, who value its life-sustaining waters. Many Hindus bathe in the river daily for spiritual purification. To learn more about the unique dolphin that inhabits the Ganges River, visit vgsbooks.com.

The **Indus River** originates high in the Himalayas and flows 1,800 miles (2,897 km) into the Arabian Sea. Most of this river, which gives India its name, lies in Pakistan.

Rivers crisscross the Deccan Plateau, providing water for crops and hydroelectric power. In addition to the Narmada, the Mahanadi River rises in the Vindhya Mountains and flows through the state of Orissa. Farther south, the Godavari River begins near the city of Mumbai and wends its way toward the Bay of Bengal. The Krishna River begins in the Western Ghats and drains into the Bay of Bengal, as does the Cauvery River.

Climate

India is so large that it contains a wide range of climates. The northern third of the country, which includes the Himalayas, experiences seasonal temperatures and cool winters. In the rest of India, temperatures range from warm to hot throughout the year. April and May are the hottest months. The temperature can reach 120°F (49°C) in the inland areas and 105°F (40°C) in the northern plains. In the south, summer temperatures average about 100°F (38°C).

Humidity and rainfall levels also vary throughout India. The rainy season begins in late May or early June, when moisture-bearing winds arrive from the Arabian Sea, hitting the southern part of the country first and moving north. These seasonal winds, called the southwest monsoon, are responsible for India's distinct rainy and dry periods. A second monsoon, called the northeast or retreating monsoon, arrives from the Bay of Bengal in October and November. The monsoons often bring torrential rains, severe storms, and flooding.

India has a diverse wildlife population, which includes tigers and monkeys. The Bengal Tiger *(left)* makes up two-thirds of the world's tiger population. The langur monkey *(below)* is sacred.

The southwestern coast and the far northeastern corner of the country, east of Bangladesh, receive the heaviest rainfall—more than 100 inches (254 centimeters) annually. The eastern half of the Indo-Gangetic Plain is also rainy, with 40 to 80 inches (102 to 204 cm) annually. Most of the Deccan Plateau has moderate precipitation, while the arid Thar Desert gets less than 10 inches (25 cm) of rainfall a year.

Flora and Fauna

India's megadiverse natural environment includes more than 45,000 species of plants, 16 major forest types, and 8,100 species of animals. Flora in India are adapted to a variety of climate and soil conditions. Where rainfall is heavy—in the Western Ghats and the northeastern states, for example—a few tropical rain forests remain, supporting evergreen, bamboo, and teak trees. Cinnamon, chestnut, birch, and plum trees grow in the monsoon-soaked foothills of the Himalayas. The moist regions give way to swampy lowlands where mangrove thickets thrive. In the hot, dry regions of the country, the natural vegetation, such as the acacia shrub, must be drought resistant to survive.

Among the animals found in India are tigers—the national animal—monkeys, camels, antelopes, and wild boars. The Ganges River is home to a rare type of dolphin that never goes into the sea.

India has turned much of its grassland and forests into farmland to feed its large population. As a result, animal habitats are becoming scarce, and the number of large mammals is dwindling. Lions, tigers, snow leopards, Indian (also called Asian) elephants, and one-horned rhinoceroses are all in danger of becoming extinct on the subcontinent.

More than 1,200 kinds of birds live in India, including the national bird, the peacock. Reptile species are also numerous. Three varieties of crocodiles inhabit India's rivers, and snakes are common.

Every year poachers capture many animals and reptiles and sell them for their fur, bones, skin, and other parts. Conservation organizations have launched efforts to protect endangered species, and the Indian government has set aside 80 national parks, 440 wildlife sanctuaries, and 23 tiger reserves.

Natural Resources and the Environment

India has rich reserves of coal, iron ore, limestone, chromite, bauxite, manganese, and other minerals. Coal is India's main source of energy, and huge coal deposits lie in Bihar, Orissa, and Madhya Pradesh. Oil drilling takes place off the shore of Mumbai, where India's main petroleum deposits are located. Other oil fields are in Assam and Gujarat. A number of precious metals and stones are mined in India, including diamonds, emeralds, gold, and silver.

Deforestation has claimed much of India's woodlands. Only about 20 percent of the country remains forested, and each year more trees are cut down than are planted. Deforestation happens for several reasons. Many trees are cut to meet the demand for farmland, and millions of people depend on wood for fuel. Valuable hardwoods such as teak, sal, and rosewood are cut for timber. Government-sponsored and grassroots conservation movements are working to restore Indian forests, but the varied types of original trees are often replaced by fast-growing eucalyptus or pine trees.

Trees

Trees feature prominently in Indian mythology and Hindu scripture. Indian tribal people regard trees as the mother who provides food, air, nourishment, fuel, and housing materials.

Because of this special regard for trees, deforestation destroys more than just forests. It strikes at the heart of Indian culture. Many environmental groups, government programs, and communities in India are working to replant forests. There is even a national tree-planting festival, the Van Mahotsava.

Clean **drinking water** is in short supply in India, especially in rural areas. The country has created programs to save water, including recycling water, growing crops that require less water, and collecting rainwater.

Fishing takes place all along India's long coastline in such states as Andhra Pradesh, Kerala, Orissa, Tamil Nadu, and West Bengal. Pollution from pesticides and other toxic chemicals has reduced fish populations near large coastal cities such as Mumbai and Kolkata, however.

An important natural resource that is in short supply is clean drinking water. One in four Indians has no access to clean, safe water, and 90 percent of water resources are polluted. Groundwater, the source of many people's drinking water, is being used up at an alarming rate.

Other environmental problems include soil erosion, air pollution, and overpopulation. Overuse of pesticides has destroyed soil, contributing to a loss of 25 billion tons (22.7 billion metric tons) of topsoil between 1996 and 2001. Air pollution from industry and vehicles is a serious problem in most of India's major cities. Delhi, with a population of about 12 million people, has some of the world's worst smog.

India is also a growing producer of greenhouse gases, carbon emissions that are thought to contribute to global warming. To produce electricity, Indian companies burn coal, an inefficient fuel that produces these gases.

Government agencies, nongovernmental organizations, and local communities are working on ways to reduce pollution and promote clean energy development and efficient energy use. Meeting these environmental challenges will be crucial for India's future health and stability.

States

India is made up of twenty-nine states and six union territories. In the 1950s, the states were reorganized according to language boundaries. For example, in the southern state of Tamil Nadu, most people speak Tamil, while in the northeastern state of Assam, the main language is Assamese. The three newest states, Chhatisgarh, Uttaranchal, and Jharkhand, were formed in November 2000.

The most densely populated states are those in the Ganges River delta and valley—Uttar Pradesh, West Bengal, and Bihar—as well as Maharashtra, where Mumbai is located. The least populated states are in the northeast corner of the country; Goa, a tiny state on the west coast; and the union territories.

Cities

India has more than twenty-five cities with populations that exceed one million. Yet less than one-third of the nation's inhabitants live in cities. Most Indians live in rural villages.

MUMBAI Formerly called Bombay, Mumbai is the largest city in India and the third largest metropolitan area in the world, with a population of more than 18 million. The city, a major port on the western coast, is an island that is linked to the mainland by many bridges. Large expanses of sea and swamps were filled in to join the original seven islands.

Mumbai is an island. The city's harbor is one of largest natural harbors in the world. Hundreds of vessels, from large freighters to small fishing boats and sailboats, use the harbor daily.

Mumbai is the financial center of India and the most industrialized city in the country. Important industries include textiles, chemicals, metals, automobiles, electronics, engineering, food processing, and publishing. The large Hindi-language film industry is also centered in Mumbai—often referred to as Bollywood.

Wealthy residents of Mumbai live in modern apartments in the city's older sections, which also contain historical and commercial landmarks from its early history as a British trading center. Cheap and poorly serviced housing developments surround the city, and overcrowding has resulted in slum of makeshift dwellings and thousands of homeless people.

Bombay officially became Mumbai in 1996, when the Hindu nationalist government of the state of Maharashtra decided to call the state capital by its name in the local language, Marathi. The name may derive from the Hindu goddess Mumba Devi, worshiped by the original inhabitants of Mumbai. Two other major cities, Kolkata and Chennai—formerly Calcutta and Madras—also changed their names in recent years in a nationalist move to reclaim their precolonial identity.

KOLKATA Lying in northeastern India along the Bay of Bengal, Kolkata, formerly Calcutta, is India's second largest city, with 12.9 million people. Kolkata is a busy port city, exporting jute (a fiber used in rope making), crude steel, iron, coal, machinery, sugar, and tea. Important industries include food processing, textiles, and iron and steel goods. The city is also the financial headquarters for eastern India.

Kolkata is known as the cultural capital of India. It is a hub of activities and festivals devoted to music, dancing, theater, and other arts. The city's citizens are also famous for their passion for sports, especially soccer and cricket. Like other large cities in India, however, Kolkata is plagued by overcrowding, poverty, and neglect. Religious and political riots have erupted in the city frequently in the last few decades.

DELHI Delhi is the capital of India and its third largest city, with a population of nearly 12 million. The metropolitan area includes Old Delhi, an ancient city that was the capital of Muslim India between the 1600s and 1800s, and New Delhi, which is just south of the old city and became India's capital in 1931. The narrow streets of the crowded old city contrast sharply with the wide thoroughfares and

Too narrow for heavy automobile traffic, the streets of **Old Delhi** are often crowded with pedestrians as well as cycle- and auto-rickshaws.

modern buildings of New Delhi. Poorer suburbs and slums are spreading along the edges of the city.

An important travel gateway and industrial hub in northwestern India, Delhi also produces manufactured goods. The city is choked by air pollution, much of it caused by the increasing automobile traffic. The government has taken steps to improve air quality, but progress has been slow.

HYDERABAD Muslim ruler Muhammad Quli Qutb Shah established Hyderabad as a capital in 1589, and the city features beautiful Islamic architecture, including palaces and mosques. With 6.8 million people, Hyderabad is a center of trade and commerce, as well as handicrafts such as jewelry, boxes, clothing, brass, toys, and carpets.

CHENNAI Located in the state of Tamil Nadu, Chennai (formerly Madras) has a population of 6.6 million and is a chief port on India's southeastern coast. Chennai contains many industrial plants, such as auto assembly facilities, cotton mills, and leather tanneries. Other industrial products include cement, glass, rubber, fertilizer, and iron.

BANGALORE With a population of 5.5 million, Bangalore is one of the fastest-growing cities in India. As the nerve center of India's thriving software industry, it is known as the Silicon Valley of India. Other major industries include aircraft, electronics, and machine tools. Bangalore is an elegant city with many parks, gardens, and tree-lined avenues.

HISTORY AND GOVERNMENT

India's history stretches back many thousands of years. Archaeological evidence shows that communities of humans lived in India around 4000 B.C. India's ancient civilizations produced cities and villages, cultivated fields, and great works of art. Over time, many different kingdoms and conquerors controlled various parts of the subcontinent.

Early Civilizations

Large-scale settlement of the Indian subcontinent occurred about 2500 B.C. along the fertile banks of the Indus River and its tributaries. A complex urban civilization grew in this region, which included present-day Pakistan and western India. Archaeologists have uncovered more than three hundred well-designed cities that featured unique architectural styles and languages. The two main urban centers were Mohenjo-Daro and Harappa, both in eastern Pakistan.

The Indus Valley civilization used standardized weights and measures and produced surplus crops to trade. Its cities had extensive

drainage systems, well-defined neighborhoods, and fortified administrative headquarters. The Indus Valley people also had a complex picture writing system. Environmental disasters such as flooding and earthquakes caused the Indus civilization to decline about 1800 B.C.

Arriving from south-central Asia between 2000 and 1000 B.C., a group of people called Aryans took control of the Ganges River basin. To escape Aryan power, most of the local inhabitants, called Dravidians, moved into southern India.

The Aryans developed a philosophical and social system that involved the worship of several gods and the division of citizens into rigid social and professional groups, or castes. The Aryans brought iron tools, the horse and chariot, and knowledge of astronomy and mathematics to the region. In addition, they wrote sacred Sanskrit-language texts known as the Vedas, which, along with later writings, form the scriptures of the Hindu religion.

Buddhists believe that Siddhartha Gautama (Buddha) attained enlightenment, or supreme spiritual wisdom and peace, after resisting temptation while meditating under a bodhi (banyan) tree in what is now northern India. Buddha, or "awakened one," first shared his teachings in India around 500 B.C.

Sixteen separate states arose in the Aryan territory during the next thousand years. These realms stretched across the northern plain from modern Afghanistan to Bangladesh and were closely tied to the Hindu religion.

By about the middle of the sixth century B.C., the Magadha kingdom had emerged as the dominant Aryan state. In the fifth century, two religious reform movements, both offshoots of Hinduism, took root in India. Siddhartha Gautama (Buddha) preached his first sermons in India around 500 B.C., leading to the foundation of Buddhism. Vardhamana Mahavira established Jainism at around the same time.

The Maurya Dynasty and the Golden Age

The Magadha ruler Chandragupta Maurya came to power in 321 B.C. and founded a dynasty (family of rulers) that governed nearly all of India for about a century. The most famous Mauryan ruler was Chandragupta's grandson Ashoka, who reigned from 272 to 232 B.C. He made Buddhism the official religion of India and renounced force as a means of governing. Ashoka's laws, which were carved on huge pillars, focused on social duty and emphasized tolerance and harmony.

Following the bloody and horrific Kalinga War (261 B.C.), victor King Ashoka dramatically renounced warfare and converted to Buddhism. Under his leadership, the peaceful teachings of Buddhism spread throughout much of India.

Within a century of Ashoka's death in 232 B.C., the Mauryan Empire declined, and no lasting regional power arose in the north for several centuries. Nevertheless, trade routes developed between India and the Persian, Chinese, and Roman Empires.

The separate kingdoms that followed the death of Ashoka came together in the fourth and fifth centuries A.D. under a new Hindu dynasty, the Guptas. The period of Gupta rule is called the golden age of India, because it fostered discoveries in mathematics, astronomy, and the arts. Scholars compiled dictionaries in Sanskrit, the language of wealthy people at the time, which later evolved into Hindi and other modern Indian languages. The caste system continued to preserve strong social divisions.

Invasions by Huns, warriors from central Asia, weakened the Gupta Empire in the second half of the fifth century. By the seventh century, many smaller Hindu kingdoms were competing for territory throughout northern India.

Muslim Rule

Over the next five hundred years, followers of the Islamic religion, called Muslims, came to control northern India through a series of military and cultural conquests. The Muslims began arriving in India soon after the death of the prophet Muhammad, the founder of Islam, in A.D. 632.

In A.D. 1000, the Muslim ruler Mahmud of Ghazni launched the first of more than fifteen military invasions into India. The disunited Indians of the northern plain were unable to resist the attacks, and by 1025 Mahmud had added the Punjab region to his empire. A Turkish ruler named Muizz-ud-din Muhammad (or Muhammad of Ghur) completed the Muslim conquest of India in 1192. He established his capital at Delhi and went on to subdue northern India as far east as Bengal. Five dynasties of the Delhi sultanate (kingdom) ruled northern India between 1206 and 1526.

The Lodi Tombs were built between 1421 and 1526, during the rule of the Delhi sultanate. The Muslim tombs, set in a grand garden, housed dead rulers from the Lodi and Sayyid dynasties.

Timur the Lame (Tamerlane), so named for a leg injury he received in youth, conquered northern India and much of central Asia before his death in 1405.

During this 320-year period, clashes often occurred between Muslim and Hindu populations. Occasionally, the two cultures blended successfully. Other times, distrust simmered between them.

The Delhi sultanate slowly declined after 1398, when the Mongol conqueror Timur the Lame (Tamerlane) swept down from central Asia and sacked Delhi. The sultanate survived for one more century before falling in 1526 to Zahir-ud-din Muhammad (Babur), a descendant of Timur.

Developments in Southern India

Southern India, situated far from the mountain passes where invaders entered the subcontinent from central Asia, enjoyed greater peace and stability over the centuries than the north did. On the Deccan Plateau, a large, strong state formed in the third century B.C. under the rule of the Andhra (or Shatavahana) dynasty. Thirty successive Andhra kings reigned from 230 B.C. to about A.D. 230, the longest continuous dynasty ever to rule in India. After the dynasty's collapse, southern India became a mosaic of small kingdoms.

In the southernmost part of India, three Dravidian kingdoms fought for power. The Cholas eventually emerged as the strongest group. They expanded their empire to include the islands of Sri Lanka and the Maldives in the tenth and eleventh centuries A.D. The Chola dynasty gave way to that of the Vijayanagars. Founded in 1336, this powerful Hindu kingdom depended on its commercial contacts, trading centers, and network of roads for its economic and political survival.

In 1347 the Bahmani kingdom, an offshoot of the Muslim Delhi sultanate, emerged in the south. The Bahmanis' efforts to expand their holdings led to frequent conflicts with the Vijayanagar kingdom. In 1565 five Muslim states formed from the Bahmani kingdom joined together to defeat the Vijayanagars, fighting a final battle at Talikota. Weakened by warfare, the kingdoms of the southern peninsula, like those of the northern plain, came under the rule of Mongol invaders from central Asia.

The Mughal Empire

Zahir-ud-din Muhammad, called Babur by his followers, united northern India under his rule between 1526 and 1530 and laid the foundations of the Mughal Empire. (The name *Mughal* is derived from the word *Mongol.*) The new Muslim leaders were talented administrators, military leaders, and diplomats. The empire traded heavily and generated immense wealth. The Mughals' religious tolerance calmed the Hindus, who initially feared the Muslim rulers would try to convert them.

The empire reached its peak under Babur's grandson Akbar, who reigned from 1556 to 1605 over an area that included nearly all of present-day India. The emperor sought the goodwill of the Hindus and placed some of them in high positions in his government.

During the reign of a later Mughal emperor, Shah Jahan, Indian architecture and art flourished. A famous example of Mughal architecture is the Taj Mahal, which the emperor had built as a mausoleum (aboveground tomb) for his favorite wife.

Twenty thousand workers built the **Taj Mahal** over sixteen years (1632–1648). Palacelike, the famous site is actually the tomb of Mughal ruler Shah Jahan and his favorite wife, Mumtaz Mahal ("Elect of the Palace").

> Visit vgsbooks.com for links to websites where you can take a virtual tour of the Taj Mahal and learn more about an ancient Indus River Valley civilization, Mughal art, and the Indian government.

Shah Jahan's son, Aurangzeb, drove his father from the throne in 1658. Aurangzeb spent twenty years trying to subdue the Hindu Marathas, a well-organized confederacy of fighters in western India and the Deccan states in the south. After Aurangzeb's death in 1707, the Mughal Empire began to decline.

The Arrival of the Europeans

After the Portuguese navigator Vasco da Gama visited India in 1498, Portuguese merchants created trade links with India, bringing goods from Europe throughout the 1500s. Reports of the wealth of Akbar's empire stirred Britain, France, and the Netherlands to compete with Portugal for India's trade.

In the seventeenth century, with the permission of Mughal emperors, the British East India Company established several trading posts in India—at Surat in 1612, Madras in 1640, Bombay in 1668, and Calcutta in 1690. The French also managed to acquire a share of the Indian trade, claiming Pondichéry (now Pondicherry) in 1670. The Mughal emperors and the trading companies both profited from the exchange of spices and textiles.

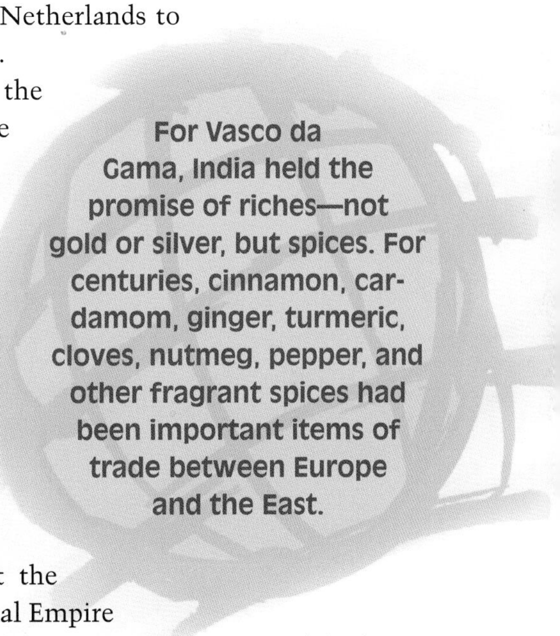

For Vasco da Gama, India held the promise of riches—not gold or silver, but spices. For centuries, cinnamon, cardamom, ginger, turmeric, cloves, nutmeg, pepper, and other fragrant spices had been important items of trade between Europe and the East.

The situation changed suddenly at the beginning of the 1700s, when the Mughal Empire began to decline. Regional rivalries erupted all over India. Fearful of losing their commercial arrangements, Britain and France made alliances with Indian princes to expel other European powers from India. The Indian princes, in turn, took advantage of the rivalry between the British and the French to gain power over other Indian rulers.

By the mid-1700s, India was a chaotic battleground where the British and French fought each other and Indian princes jockeyed for control. Under the leadership of Robert Clive, British forces defeated the French in 1751, and in 1757 they overcame the ruler of Bengal at the Battle of Plassey (now called Palashi).

Tipu Sultan is depicted in this mural leading Indian soldiers against British forces about 1790. Tipu and other sultans opposed the British Empire's increasing control in India and fought for independence during the Mysore Wars (1767–1799).

For the next hundred years, Great Britain steadily extended its influence, and by the mid-1800s, officials of the East India Company held political and economic power across nearly the entire subcontinent. In May 1857, however, rebellions against British control broke out in Bengal and central India. (Indian nationalists called the conflict the First War of Independence, while the British referred to it as the Sepoy Mutiny.) Although the revolt had many causes, a major one was Indian objections to British attempts to convert Hindus and Muslims to Christianity.

After ten months of fighting, British troops defeated the rebels. Britain then transferred administrative responsibility for India from the East India Company to the British government.

British India

The monarch of Britain at the time, Queen Victoria, became empress of India and appointed a viceroy to represent her as head of the Indian government. British India was referred to as the Raj. (*Raj* means "rule" or "kingdom" in Hindi.) Officials of the British government indirectly ruled the Indian states, and treaties existed between local princes and the British.

The British built extensive railway, road, and telegraph networks, widened irrigation systems, and provided food relief during famines. Britain used India as a source of raw materials and as a market for British-manufactured goods but made little effort to help India remain economically independent. As a result, India's once self-sufficient economy became tied to markets over which it had no control.

Under British rule, discrimination against Indians was far-reaching. All Indians—even those who were wealthy and well educated—were barred from social contact with the British. Only British men could serve as officers in the Indian army. These divisions helped stimulate nationalist feelings among Indians.

The Road to Independence

As opposition to British rule grew, a group of Indian lawyers and other professionals formed the Indian National Congress in 1885. The original aim of the Congress was to have more participation by Indians in the country's government.

Some Muslims in India believed that the Indian National Congress was a strictly Hindu organization that aimed to establish a Hindu government. With the support of the British, who feared that the Congress would become too powerful, Muslim leaders created the Muslim League in 1906 to ensure their place in Indian politics.

During World War I (1914–1918), more than one million Indian soldiers fought with British troops in Europe and the Middle East. India cooperated with Britain partly because the British promised increased self-government for Indians after the war. But the Government of India Act of 1919 made few changes. Thousands of Indians demonstrated in protest on April 13, 1919, in Amritsar. British troops fired on the crowds, killing more than 300 people and wounding about 1,200 others.

Following the Amritsar Massacre, a British-trained Indian lawyer named Mohandas K. Gandhi (later also called Mahatma, the "Great Soul") became leader of the Indian National Congress. His policy of nonviolent resistance gained many supporters. Gandhi encouraged the boycott of foreign-made goods and the local production of textiles.

Gandhi's philosophy, called *satyagraha,* loosely translated as "moral domination," involved disobeying laws that he believed were

One of Mohandas Gandhi's most famous acts of civil disobedience, the **Salt March,** occurred in 1930. Gandhi *(with walking stick)* led several thousand protesters to the seaside village of Dandi on India's west coast. There, in defiance of a hated British tax on salt, he made salt by evaporating seawater.

discriminatory or immoral and accepting arrest for having broken the laws. His approach also included fasting as a means of protest. Since Gandhi's followers were unarmed and peaceful, the British were reluctant to attack them and usually only sent them to prison.

The Indian National Congress attracted many Indians and developed a pan-Indian approach—that is, it sought to unite religious, language, and ethnic groups. In contrast, the Muslim League, led by Mohammad Ali Jinnah, demanded a separate Muslim voter roll and a guaranteed place for Muslims in any future independent India movement.

After negotiating with various Indian leaders, Britain passed a new Government of India Act in 1935. The plan established fairly independent provincial governments. Members of the Indian National Congress dominated these regional councils.

In 1939 Britain declared itself and its empire, including India, at war with Germany. Because Britain had not involved the Indian National Congress in making this decision, the Congress refused to cooperate with the British during World War II. As an act of protest, Congress leaders withdrew completely from provincial government. The British response was to jail the Congress leaders for the duration of the war.

The Muslim League, on the other hand, fully supported Britain during World War II. The league hoped to gain recognition for the rights of the Muslim community. In 1940 Jinnah called for the creation of a separate Muslim nation.

After the war ended in 1945, Britain's economy was weak and its army was ready to go home. The British could neither financially support their empire nor police it. The time had come for Indian independence.

At first the British tried to find common ground between the Indian National Congress and the Muslim League. But the split between the two groups was so great that they could not agree on a form of post-independence government. Partition, or division of India into two separate nations for Hindus and Muslims, appeared to be the only solution.

Partition and Independence

In June 1947, Britain announced a plan to divide the subcontinent into two countries—India, with a Hindu majority, and Pakistan, with a Muslim majority. The princely states (states ruled by princes) could join either nation or remain independent.

The Congress Party, as the Indian National Congress became known, and the Muslim League agreed to the plan, and in August 1947, Britain formally acknowledged India and Pakistan as independent nations. Massive migrations of refugees began immediately. Hindus living in Pakistan moved to India, and Muslims in India traveled to West Pakistan or East Pakistan, the two wings of the new Muslim state. Riots and violence occurred in many large cities, and harassment of religious minorities in both countries forced many people to flee to safety.

BLOODY PARTITION

Neatly slicing India and Pakistan into two countries based on religion proved to be a painful and bloody task. Although some areas were clearly Hindu or Muslim, others had mixed populations. The decision about where to draw the borders was fraught with impossible dilemmas.

Partition took place on August 14, 1947. For the next several months, a great exodus took place across the subcontinent, as Muslims in India fled to Pakistan and Hindus and Sikhs fled to India. Trains full of Muslims were stopped and the passengers killed by Hindu and Sikh mobs, while Muslim mobs attacked Hindus and Sikhs fleeing in the other direction.

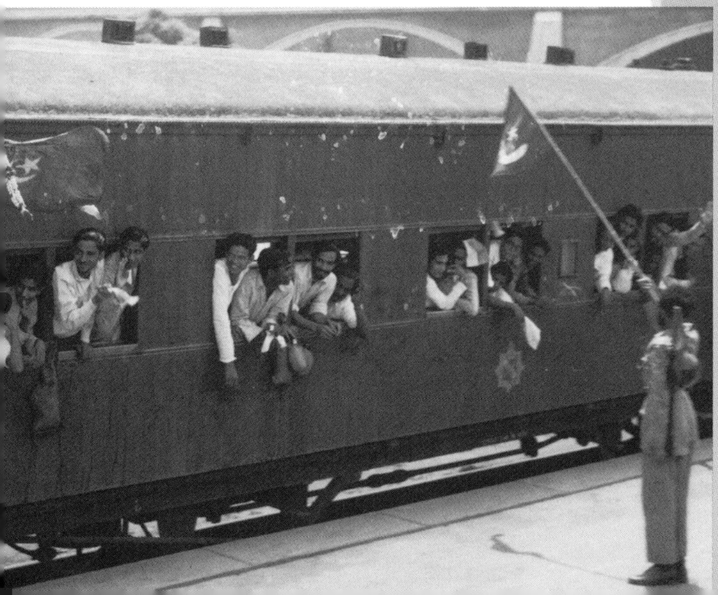

Muslims crowd a train leaving Delhi bound for Pakistan in 1947.

During this period, Mohandas Gandhi urged understanding and nonviolence. A Hindu who believed Gandhi was too tolerant of Muslims assassinated him in 1948.

"Intolerance is itself a form of violence and an obstacle to the growth of a true democratic spirit."

–Mohandas K. Gandhi

One of the first tasks of the new Indian government was to unify the separate states. The central government persuaded many princes to join the new nation by retaining them as ceremonial heads of state and paying them yearly pensions.

Jammu and Kashmir, a Muslim state ruled by a Hindu prince, refused at first to join either India or Pakistan. Muslim troops from Pakistan poured into the region, and Pakistan claimed the state. Kashmir's ruler responded by joining the Indian union. The war continued until 1949, when the United Nations arranged a cease-fire. Since then, both India and Pakistan have claimed the territory.

India's first prime minister was Jawaharlal Nehru, a Congress Party member who had been a close associate of Gandhi. India's Constitution went into effect on January 26, 1950, establishing the country as a republic. Later reorganizations eliminated the power of the princes and created new states.

National Development

After independence, Nehru launched a plan for economic development. He wanted to use government money to improve irrigation techniques, to build hydroelectric power plants, and to broaden the transportation network. With public funds, he encouraged Indian manufacturers to produce items that India had previously imported. As a result, India began to make its own heavy machinery and weapons. Agricultural production also increased.

In the 1950s and 1960s, Nehru, along with Tito of Yugoslavia and Sukarno of Indonesia, brought together nations that sought political independence. These leaders formed the Nonaligned Movement, whose goal was to avoid control by either of the world's superpowers, the United States and the Soviet Union.

In spite of successes at the international level, Nehru faced troubles along India's own borders. In December 1961, Indian troops invaded and eventually took over the small Portuguese territories of Goa, Daman, and Diu in coastal areas of southern India. In 1962 border wars with China broke out in the Himalayas, resulting in Chinese troops overrunning Indian outposts. The situation remained tense until China declared a cease-fire later that year.

The daughter of **Jawaharlal Nehru** *(left)*, **Indira Gandhi** *(right)* followed in her father's footsteps, becoming India's prime minister in 1966. Nehru was the first prime minister of India, and Gandhi was its first female prime minister.

The Rise of Indira Gandhi

After Nehru's death in 1964, border conflicts between India and Pakistan intensified into a war in 1965. Nehru's successor, Lal Bahadur Shastri, eased the confrontation through a Soviet-sponsored cease-fire. A few hours after signing the peace agreement in January 1966, Shastri died of a heart attack. After some political infighting, Nehru's daughter Indira Gandhi (no relation to Mohandas Gandhi) became prime minister.

Civil war broke out between West and East Pakistan in 1971, spurred by a movement by the Bengali people in East Pakistan to establish a homeland called Bangladesh. Millions of East Pakistani refugees fled to India. Air raids into India from East Pakistan provoked an invasion by Indian troops, which quickly defeated West Pakistan's forces. Soon afterward, East Pakistan declared itself the independent Republic of Bangladesh.

In mid-1975, several opposition parties combined to call for Indira Gandhi's resignation. In addition, India's highest court declared her guilty of election violations in 1971 and barred her from Parliament for six years. Gandhi's response was to declare a state of emergency, which made it legal for her to suspend the Constitution and jail those opposed to her policies.

Gandhi's harsh measures met with strong resistance. Her imprisonment of respected political figures, such as Morarji Desai, made her extremely unpopular. In 1977 the prime minister dissolved the legislature and called national elections, in which she and her party were badly defeated. Morarji Desai became prime minister as the head of the new Janata party, an alliance of four anti-Gandhi groups.

The Desai coalition suffered from political infighting, however, and it fell apart in December 1979.

The Modern Era

Elections in 1980 brought Indira Gandhi back to power as prime minister. The legal actions against her were dropped. Gandhi's son Sanjay, who was being prepared to succeed his mother, died in a plane crash in 1980. Thereafter, Indira Gandhi's hopes for continuing her policies came to rest on her other son, Rajiv.

During the next few years, protests in Assam and in the Sikh community of Punjab ended in violence. In 1984 militant Sikh separatists, demanding a separate Sikh state, occupied the Golden Temple at Amritsar, a revered shrine for people who follow the Sikh religion. Government troops were sent in to dislodge the militants. Several hundred people were killed, and the sacred site was seriously damaged. Angered by the attack, two of the prime minister's Sikh bodyguards assassinated Indira Gandhi in October 1984, and Rajiv Gandhi became the premier. General elections soon followed, and the new prime minister, Gandhi, won the largest majority of any political leader in Indian history.

By 1986, however, Punjab had nearly disintegrated into civil war, and several members of Gandhi's inner circle were involved in a number of scandals. As a result, his popular support declined, and his party was defeated in elections in 1989.

V. P. Singh, the head of the National Front, a coalition of anti-Gandhi and anticorruption groups, became prime minister in December 1989. Despite the change in leadership, violence and loss of life still rocked India. Sikhs in Punjab, Assamese in Assam, and Kashmiris in Jammu and Kashmir expressed their desire for independence through public demonstrations, bombings, and guerrilla tactics. Indian soldiers called in to establish order in these states also contributed to the violence.

In November 1990, after less than a year in office, Singh got a no-confidence vote in the Indian legislature and had to resign. A minority administration took over as a caretaker government until elections could be held in May 1991. In late May, while campaigning in southern India, Rajiv Gandhi was assassinated.

After the election, Congress Party leader P. V. Narasimha Rao became prime minister. Rao began his term by addressing economic problems such as a soaring foreign debt and declining economic growth. Regulations were passed to reserve 27 percent of government jobs for lower-caste people, in addition to the 22.5 percent set aside for "untouchables" (Scheduled Castes) and tribal people.

Continuing Challenges

The 1990s were marked by political turbulence and corruption, rising tensions between Muslims and Hindus, and ongoing conflict with Pakistan in the Kashmir region. In 1992 the Bharatiya Janata Party (BJP), a Hindu nationalist political party, helped organize militants to construct a Hindu temple on the site of the Babri Masjid, a sixteenth-century Islamic mosque in Ayodhya in the state of Uttar Pradesh. (Hindus had destroyed the mosque in October 1990 because they said it had been built over the birthplace of the god Rama.) This gesture insulted Muslims throughout India. Rioting and violence flared in Mumbai and other parts of India, and anti-Hindu demonstrations were held in Pakistan and Bangladesh.

Kocheril Narayanan

Prime Minister Rao held onto power until 1996, when inconclusive results in the general election led to a political free-for-all. No party won an overall majority in Parliament, and several parties tried to form a new government. During the next two years, four different governments held—and lost—power. In July 1997, Kocheril Raman Narayanan was elected president, a notable appointment since he was the first untouchable, or Dalit, to become president of India.

During the general election of 1998, Sonia Gandhi, Rajiv Gandhi's widow, campaigned on behalf of the Congress Party and later became the party's president. In the election, however, the Congress Party did poorly, and the BJP emerged as the predominant force in Indian politics. BJP leader Atal Bihari Vajpayee became prime minister, leading a coalition government.

Soon after Vajpayee came to power, his government shocked India and the rest of the world by carrying out a series of underground nuclear test explosions in the deserts of Rajasthan. Any hope of a peaceful resolution to the conflict over Kashmir was shattered as Pakistan responded with nuclear tests of its own. The United States and other countries condemned the tests and imposed economic sanctions on India and Pakistan. Nonetheless, Vajpayee was reelected in October 1999, and the BJP secured a comfortable majority in Parliament.

Atal Vajpayee

Fighting in the Kashmir region continued to flare up during the 1990s and early 2000s. In 1996 the total death toll resulting from the conflict in

Jammu and Kashmir was estimated at twenty thousand. Indian police recorded nearly four thousand violent incidents in 2001, including two terrorist attacks by Islamic fundamentalists in October 2001.

The India-Pakistan conflict drew increased international attention after September 11, 2001, when Islamic fundamentalist terrorists attacked the World Trade Center and the Pentagon in the United States, killing thousands of people. The United States went to war against the Taliban rulers of Afghanistan, accused of harboring the terrorist leaders behind the September 11 attack. To gain the cooperation and support of India and Pakistan in the war in Afghanistan, the United States lifted economic sanctions against India and Pakistan.

U.S. Secretary of State Colin Powell traveled to India in October 2001 as part of this effort. Declaring that the United States and India were united against terrorism, Powell pledged that the United States would help resolve the Kashmir conflict. India cooperated with the United States in the war by sharing intelligence information about Islamic extremists in Pakistan and Afghanistan and allowing U.S. forces to use air space over India. In December 2001, the United States and India announced agreements to move forward with joint military exercises and U.S. military sales to India. Military officials from both countries said they would work together to counter threats of international terrorism, narcotics trafficking, and other threats.

Indian soldiers on patrol in the Jammu and Kashmir region. Tensions are ongoing between India and Pakistan over disputed borders in the region.

Nonetheless, continuing violence in 2002 led to a military buildup along the border and a standoff that brought the two countries to the brink of another war. In response to the flare-up of violence, Secretary Powell and other international officials traveled to the region to encourage the leaders of India and Pakistan to find a peaceful solution to the conflict, including open elections in Kashmir. The situation, however, remains volatile and represents one of India's major challenges for the future.

Government

Under the Constitution adopted in 1950, India is a parliamentary republic. Every five years, an electoral college consisting of members of Parliament chooses a president, whose duties are essentially ceremonial. Real power is in the hands of the prime minister, who is elected by Parliament. The prime minister may dissolve Parliament and call for new elections before the end of the allotted five-year term.

Legislative power rests with a two-house Parliament that consists of the Rajya Sabha (Council of States) and the Lok Sabha (House of the People). The state legislatures elect the 245 members of the Rajya Sabha, except for 12 whom the president appoints. The 545 members of the Lok Sabha are elected by the people, except for 2 delegates who are named by the president.

India's judicial system has its roots in British law. The highest Indian tribunal is the Supreme Court, whose members are appointed to lifelong terms by the president. High, district, and magistrate courts complete the judicial structure.

State and territorial governments are structured much like the central government and have extensive authority over local affairs. These governments are responsible for education, health, and other services. On the local level, village councils, or *panchayats,* elected by the villagers serve as intermediaries between villages and state or territorial governments.

VOTING IN INDIA

In the world's largest democracy, calculating the votes of the 250 million or so people who turn up at the polls for major elections requires some tricky logistics. Long ballot papers *(below)* contain information in eighteen different languages, as well as pictorial symbols for every candidate so that voters who can't read can differentiate among candidates. A ballot paper might list more than one hundred candidates.

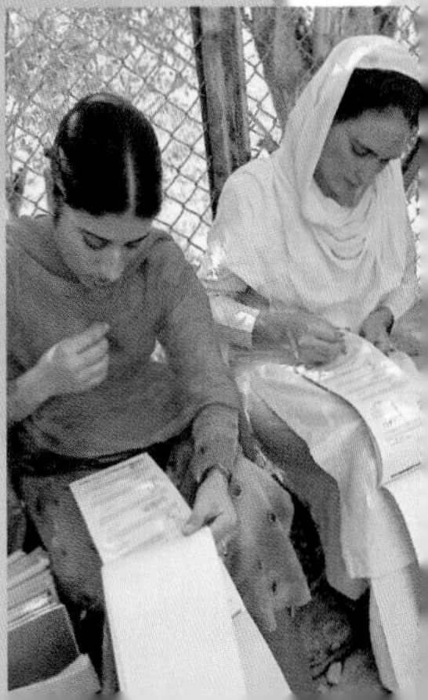

THE PEOPLE

After China, India has the largest population of any country in the world. With more than 1 billion people, India is home to one-sixth of the world's population, although it occupies only 2 percent of the world's land. Even though birth rates have declined steadily since a peak population growth rate between 1961 and 1981, the country is still growing by more than 16 million people each year. If this trend continues, India will overtake China in 2045 by reaching a population of 1.5 billion.

The current total fertility rate—the average number of children born to a woman during her lifetime—is 3.2. For India's population to stabilize, the fertility rate must drop to below 2. Concerned about overpopulation, the Indian government has had family planning programs in place since 1952 to promote the ideal of having 2 children or less per family. The national population policy aims to bring the rate to that level by 2010 and to achieve a stable population by 2045, which will allow for sustainable economic growth and social development.

Since the early 1990s, more people are choosing to limit their family size. One challenge for the government is to provide incentives to poor and illiterate people, who prefer to have as many children as they can so the children can go to work and contribute to the family income. Other population policy goals are to increase the availability of reproductive health services and contraceptives; to keep girls in school longer; and to raise the age at which women marry. Half of the young women in India are married before the legal age of 18, and the median age at first birth is 19.6 years. Women who marry and have children at a young age tend to have larger, less healthy families, according to India's National Family Health Survey.

Demographics

India's population is young—more than one-third (36 percent) of the people are under age 15. About 72 percent of the population still lives in rural communities, even though India has many large cities with growing populations. India's overall population density per square mile is 814 people (2,108 people per sq. km) but is much higher in the large cities. (By comparison, the population density of the United States is 77 people per square mile, or 199 per sq. km).

While India has a large and growing middle class, many people remain poor. In the mid-1990s, more than one-third of Indians (some 370 million people) were living below the national poverty line—the amount of money needed to buy very basic food with little money left over to buy nonfood items.

Ethnic Diversity

Various ethnic groups make up India's diverse population. The Dravidian people originally resided in northern India about four thousand years ago, during the time of the Indus civilization. After the arrival of the Aryans from central Asia, the Dravidians moved south, where their descendants form the majority ethnic group on the peninsula.

The Aryans and their descendants in the region came to be called Indo-Aryans, or Indo-Europeans. Islamic peoples arrived via Afghanistan and Iran in about A.D. 1000. They settled in the northeast, and their descendants still live in West Bengal, Uttar Pradesh, and other states in the region. The Himalayan region attracted central Asians from more remote regions.

Indo-Aryans *(left)* and Dravidians *(right)* are the two largest ethnic groups in India. Indo-Aryans make up about 72 percent of India's population. Twenty-five percent of the population is of Dravidian descent.

About 55 million people belong to tribal communities in India. Adivasis, as these people are known, have origins that date back to before the Dravidians and the Aryans. For thousands of years, they lived in the hills and forests, particularly in the northeastern part of the country. In recent years, because of increasing pressure for land, more and more Adivasis have been forced off their ancestral lands and are exploited for cheap labor in cities and villages.

The Caste System

The caste system forms the basic social structure of Hindu society. The system originated in one of the ancient sacred texts, the Rig Veda. According to the traditional framework, Hindus are born into one of four *varnas,* or castes, which were originally based loosely on occupation. The wealthiest and most prestigious group are the Brahmans (priests). In descending order of importance are the Kshatriyas (warriors and rulers), the Vaisyas (merchants and artisans), and the Sudras (servants and laborers). Within the varnas are thousands of smaller family groups.

The **Brahman Caste** is the elite caste in traditional Hindu society. In the past, Brahmans were highly respected as the priests and teachers of Indian society. The red dot *(bindi,* or "third eye") on this Brahman woman's forehead, formerly worn only by women of her caste, is a symbol of inner wisdom.

Beneath the four main castes are the untouchables, considered outside the system. Known by the government as the Scheduled Castes, they make up more than one-fifth of India's population. Mohandas Gandhi, who fought to end discrimination against untouchables, coined a new term for them—*Harijans,* meaning "people of God." These people refer to themselves as Dalits, a word that means "oppressed, downtrodden, or broken." Dalits perform the most menial jobs, such as cleaning latrines and sweeping.

"Do not believe in fate. Believe in your strength. You must abolish your slavery yourselves."

—Dr. B. R. Ambedkar, leader of untouchables

Although the Indian constitution prohibits discrimination based on caste, the system still wields influence. It has deep historical roots, supports the political structure, and helps Indians define who they are. Members of lower castes are eligible for a variety of government benefits, such as jobs and education, and they hold political power.

Traditionally, complex rules governed contact between people of different castes. For example, most people marry someone from the same caste. However, as more people enter the middle class—an aspiration shared by people from different religions, cultures, and castes—other factors, such as education, profession, and lifestyle, become more important than caste in determining social status. Modernization and urbanization have also led to a decline in the outward display of caste exclusiveness.

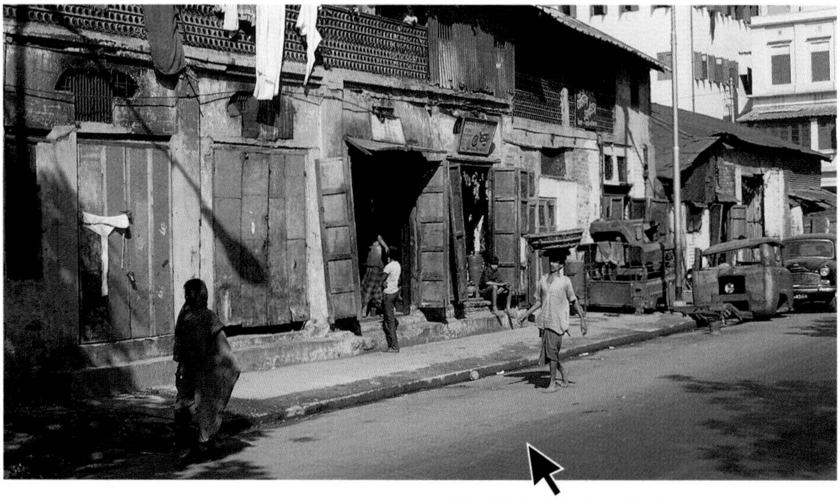

The poorest Hindus belong to the **Scheduled Castes.** Despite laws banning discrimination, bias against 260 million untouchables continues in India. To find out more about the caste system, visit vgsbooks.com.

A **medical researcher** carries out a test as part of a study on the human immunodeficiency virus (HIV), the virus that causes AIDS. Women in India's cities are moving into the professional sector in increasing numbers.

Women in Indian Society

Women have long had a disadvantaged position in Indian society. For example, women make up the largest portion of Indians living in poverty. Because girls are more likely to suffer from neglect and malnutrition in childhood, the number of deaths of girls ages one to four is estimated to be 1.5 times higher than the number of deaths among boys the same age. More boys than girls attend school, and only 54 percent of women can read and write, compared with 76 percent of men. Domestic violence against women—a subject not readily discussed in India—is thought to be pervasive.

Women in India have made some strides toward gender equality. They are living longer and are more likely to be literate than ever before. More than 1 million women have been elected to village councils, and in the cities, women are increasingly joining the ranks of working professionals.

Despite this progress, a pronounced gender imbalance is seen in the population's ratio of girls to boys. In India, the number of girls per 1,000 boys was 927 in 2001, down from 945 in 1991 and 962 in 1981. Since the 1980s, the spread of ultrasound technology has allowed parents to learn the sex of a child before birth, and unwanted daughters are regularly aborted. These sex-selective abortions are illegal, but since they are generally kept secret, enforcement of the law is weak. More girls are also neglected after birth or allowed to die. In the past, some female babies were killed.

This gender imbalance is attributed to an age-old cultural preference for sons, who carry the family name, inherit property, care for their parents in old age, and light their fathers' funeral pyres. In contrast, a girl requires the payment of a dowry upon marriage, then moves to another village to join her husband's family.

Education

Since independence, India has worked to improve the nation's educational system. The country's literacy rate has risen dramatically since 1950 and at the beginning of the 21st century stands at 76 percent for men and 54 percent for women. Education levels and literacy rates vary across the country. The southern state of Kerala, for example, has achieved the highest literacy levels.

India's schools are controlled by the states, but the national government provides financial help and centralized planning. The free educational system includes eight years of elementary classes and three of secondary schooling.

Nearly all children between the ages of 6 and 10 attend classes, but only 49 percent of older students are enrolled in school. Fewer children go to school in rural areas, where not as many schools exist and children are often put to work at a young age. More boys than girls attend school. Among children ages 11 to 14, 80 percent of boys and 67 percent of girls attend school. India has about 10,000 colleges and more than 200 universities, with enrollment of more than 7 million students.

Schoolchildren begin their day in Mangalore. The Indian constitution grants all Indian children a free education until age 14, but many rural children do not have access to schools. India is striving to ensure equal access for all students.

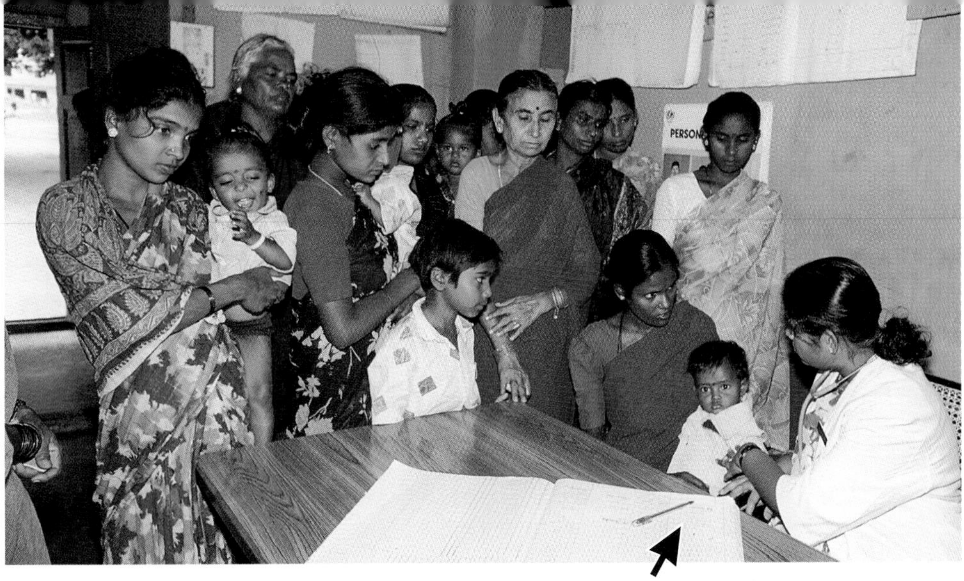

Indian women and children meet with a **health care professional.** Education and immunization programs are helping Indian families prevent illness.

Health

Despite government efforts to improve living conditions, Indians continue to suffer from poor health. Substandard diets, unsafe water, and inadequate medical facilities contribute to the nation's health risks. Infectious diseases, particularly HIV/AIDS, represent a growing threat.

The infant mortality rate—the number of infant deaths per 1,000 live births—has decreased, but it remains high. About 70 of every 1,000 Indian babies die before they reach the age of one, down from 90 ten years ago. In comparison, the U.S. infant mortality rate is 7.1 of every 1,000 births. Progress has been made in immunizing Indian children against diseases such as measles and polio, but child malnutrition remains a serious problem. Almost 50 percent of Indian children under age three are underweight, and nearly 75 percent suffer from anemia (deficiency of red blood cells, hemoglobin, or total amount of blood). Weakened by malnutrition, many children are vulnerable to dysentery and other water-borne diseases.

In 2001 life expectancy was 61 years (up from 32 in 1947). India has many health clinics, but people in rural areas have trouble reaching them because of limited numbers of clinics and limited transportation. Government-sponsored health care services have encouraged Indians to have fewer children, and about half of Indian women of child-bearing age use birth control.

Since the 1990s, AIDS has been on the rise in India. Although less than 1 percent of the population is affected, India has a higher number of HIV-infected people than most other countries in the world—an estimated 3.5 to 4 million people. Prevention efforts have focused on raising awareness, but many Indians, especially women, lack basic information about the disease. Only 4 out of 10 women of reproductive age in India have heard of AIDS.

CULTURAL LIFE

Stretching back more than five thousand years, India's culture has been enriched by successive waves of migration. India is a land of gods and goddesses, saints, gurus, and prophets, of colorful festivals and ancient arts, of sacred texts and popular movies, of countless languages and a vibrant literature.

Religion

Religion plays an important role in the lives of most Indians. More than 80 percent of India's population follows the Hindu religion, one of the world's oldest faiths. The second most common religion in India is Islam. Conflicts between Hindus and Muslims erupt frequently, generally because of differences in political goals.

Unlike many other religions, Hinduism cannot be traced to one founder, does not have just one holy book, and does not advocate the worship of one particular deity. Hindus may worship Shiva, Vishnu, Rama, Krishna, or any of thousands of gods and goddesses that may be

manifestations of Brahma, the supreme soul of the universe. In Hindu belief, all souls eventually return to and merge with Brahma. This return takes place after a person has lived through a series of earthly lives, an individual destiny called karma. The experience of living is seen as preparation for a higher existence that begins after release from the long cycle of birth, death, and rebirth.

Caste determines a person's social role and responsibilities, collectively called dharma. The fulfillment of one's dharma is considered the task of every Hindu. A fourth major concept of Hinduism is maya, the belief that the world and its people are illusions and that only the Brahma is real.

About 12 percent of India's population is Muslim. Most Muslim villages in India are made up of people from one of the two major sects of Islam, Shiism and Sunnism. Many Hindu customs and traditions survive in India's Muslim communities because of the large number of Hindu converts to Islam.

Many Sikh men have the same last name. Traditionally raised to be courageous warriors, Sikh men take the last name Singh, which means "lion."

Faithful Muslims fulfill several obligations, including daily prayer, fasting, charitable donations, and pilgrimage to the holy site of Mecca, Saudi Arabia. In large villages, mosques (Muslim places of worship) stand alongside Hindu temples.

About 35 million Indians are Christians. Part of the Christian community is made up of descendants of the Nestorians, a Christian sect that arose in the first few centuries of the Christian era. Other Indian Christians are descendants of people whom Western missionaries converted during the colonial period.

Nineteen million Sikhs and 5 million Jains—collectively about 2.5 percent of the population—follow religions that are native to India. Both faiths arose as reform sects of Hinduism. Sikhism was founded in the late 1400s by Guru Nanak to resolve the differences between Hindus and Muslims through a new religion that combined elements of both faiths. One of the original aims of Sikhism was to abolish the Hindu caste system. Most of the Sikh community lives in the Punjab region in northern India, particularly the Sikh state of Haryana.

These Indian women are attending a **Muslim wedding.** In celebration of the festive occasion, the women are wearing a colorful traditional dress called the *jilbaab*, which covers the entire body .

Mahavira (the "Great Hero") founded Jainism in the sixth century B.C. He taught that all life is sacred and urged followers to adopt a pure lifestyle. Devout Jains practice fasting and meditation, and they do not eat meat. They abstain from sexual activity and have few belongings. The Jains' strict lifestyle and reverence for living creatures receive much respect in India.

An Indian prince, Siddhartha Gautama, later called Buddha (meaning "enlightened or awakened one") established Buddhism in India in the sixth century B.C. Buddha's teaching stressed moral duties and good behavior and arose as a reaction against the complex rituals of Hinduism. In the early part of the 21st century, less than 1 percent of Indians practice the Buddhist faith.

YOGA

Yoga is a system of physical and mental discipline that dates back to the second century B.C. Yoga originated as a spiritual tradition within Hinduism, Buddhism, and Jainism. The practice developed many different branches and forms.

Yoga entered the West mainly through the missionary work of Swami Vivekananda, who spoke at the Parliament of Religions in 1893. A century later, about 20 million people in the West practice yoga. In the United States, the most popular form is hatha yoga, which involves breathing techniques, meditation, and physical postures or poses.

Languages

Although Hindi is the official language of the Republic of India, the Constitution recognizes 18 national languages, and the population speaks about 1,600 dialects. Hindi belongs to the Indo-European family of languages. Other major Indian languages in this family include Bengali, Punjabi, Urdu, Marathi, Gujarati, and Assamese. Dravidian languages such as Tamil, Kannada, Telugu, and Malayalam are spoken in southern India. English is the language of business in India and is also used in universities. Most educated Indians are multilingual.

Literature

Indian literature began with the sacred books of Hinduism, the four Vedas. Written in Sanskrit starting in about 1500 B.C., the Vedas contain Hindu law and philosophy. Indians still read the four Vedas for the ideals they express and for the beauty of the language. More famous in the Western world are India's great folk epics, which were written after the Vedas. The main epics are the Ramayana and the Mahabharata, which includes the well-known Bhagavad Gita.

Between the classic Sanskrit texts and the works of contemporary writers, Indians have produced a vast body of literature in many languages. Among modern writers, one of the most widely read is Rabindranath Tagore, a Bengali artist, poet, novelist, playwright, and songwriter who won the Nobel Prize for Literature in 1913. The novelist R. K. Narayan became well known across the world for his stories about a fictitious South Indian town called Malgudi.

Recent decades have seen a flowering of contemporary literature, much of it written in English by Indian authors living outside India. Salman Rushdie won England's Booker Prize for literature in 1981 with his novel *Midnight's Children* and later wrote the controversial novel *The Satanic Verses.* Arundhati Roy won the same prize in 1997 for her novel *The God of Small Things.* In 2001 the writer V. S. Naipaul, who was born in Trinidad of Indian descent, won the Nobel Prize for Literature. Other contemporary writers include Vikram Seth, Rohinton Mistry, Anita Desai, her daughter Kiran Desai, Amitav Ghosh, and Manil Suri.

Music and Dance

Classical Indian music has two dominant strains, the Carnatic or South Indian and the Hindustani or North Indian. Indian musicians use a variety of instruments, including the sitar, a stringed instrument, and a drum called the tabla. Classical music is enjoyed by a fairly small section of society, however. Most Indians are more familiar with their local folk music, played during festivals and ceremonies, and with pop music, especially music from "Bollywood" movies.

Dance is one of the most widely cultivated art forms in India. The two main forms are classical and folk. The gestures of the hands, the positions of the neck, and the motions of the eyes are the most striking features of Indian dance. Some dances, such as bharatanatyam in Tamil Nadu, are very old. Kathakali dancers wear heavy makeup to dramatize ancient characters, and manipuri performers sway gracefully in wide skirts.

Dance has been an important part of Indian culture for more than five thousand years. Traditional Indian dances include bharatanatyam, kathak, kathakali, kuchipudi, manipuri, mohini attam, and odissi.

Colorful, **intricate carvings** decorate a Hindu temple in Karnataka. Hindu temples are dedicated to gods such as Vishnu, Shiva *(center)*, Krishna *(bottom)*, and others.

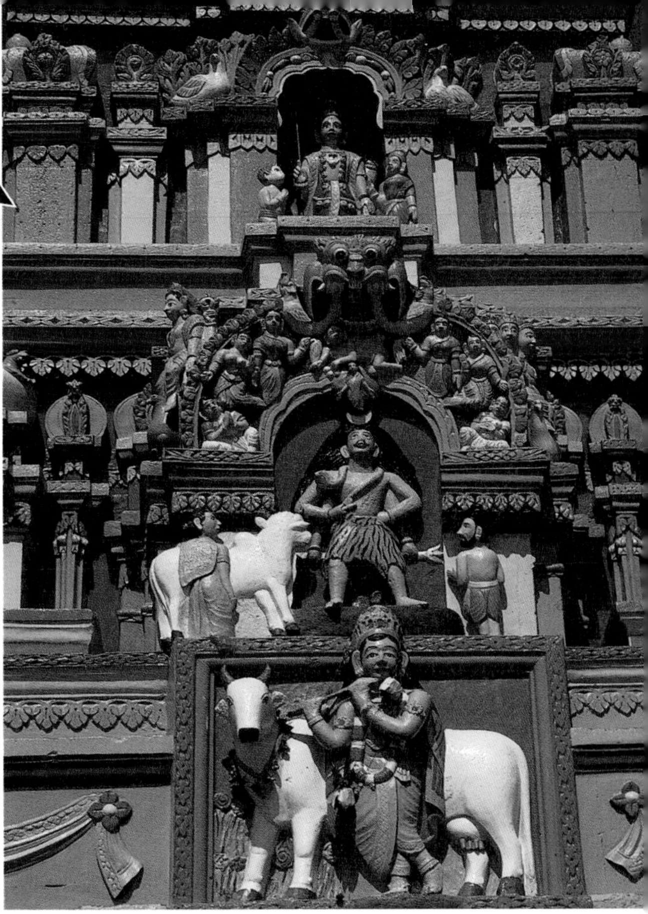

The Visual Arts

India's most famous building is the Taj Mahal. Built in the 1600s of white marble and ornamented with exquisite mosaics, it is one of the world's most beautiful buildings.

Indian classical architecture and sculpture are generally inseparable. Hindu temples were lavishly decorated with sculpture. Impressive examples are found in the great temple complexes of South India, such as Sri Meenakshi in Tamil Nadu, which is adorned with multicolored sculptures of gods and goddesses.

The most ancient paintings in India are found in the Ajanta caves in the western part of the country. The cave walls and ceilings show animals, birds, lotus flowers, and scenes from Buddha's life. The best-known style of Indian painting, delicate miniature paintings, reached its peak between the sixteenth and eighteenth centuries. These colorful paintings present a mass of small details and typically depict life within the upper levels of Indian society. Since then, Indian art has been more influenced by modern Western art.

Film and Media

India's film industry is the largest in the world, producing about eight hundred films each year. Several movies have won prizes at international film festivals. Many films, including those of the great filmmaker

"Bollywood" film sign

Satyajit Ray and contemporary director Deepa Mehta, discuss the way changes in Indian society affect everyday life. In addition to these realistic films, Bollywood churns out hundreds of blockbusters featuring wild plots, violence, car chases, jokes, and plenty of songs.

The print and electronic media are also very active in India. Approximately four thousand newspapers, including four hundred dailies, are published in more than a dozen languages. In addition, a range of magazines are available. Television is very popular, thanks to satellite and cable TV. Zee TV is a popular Hindi-language channel. The largest radio operator is All India Radio.

Sports and Games

Two of India's major sports, cricket and field hockey, were brought to the subcontinent by the British. Field hockey is the national game of India, but cricket is its obsession. Thousands of fans turn out for big games, and kids often play informal cricket games on street corners. Soccer, tennis, and horse racing also enjoy some popularity.

Two old games native to India are still played. *Kabaddi* and *kho-kho* are both vigorous versions of tag, requiring skill and strength. These ancient games are simple, fun, and cost nothing.

The game of **cricket** is played with eleven players per team. A batsman *(center)* attempts to hit a pitched ball, then runs between two bases marked by three posts called wickets. A pitcher called a bowler *(top right)* tries to "put out" batters by hitting the wickets. A team bats until ten players are put out.

Food

Indian cooking is influenced by local culture, geography, and climate. Grains, such as wheat, barley, and rice, are an important part of the diet of most Indians. Also prominent are legumes, foods that come from seed pods, such as beans, lentils, and peas. The heart of Indian cooking is the use of spices. Black mustard seeds, cardamom, chilies, coriander, cumin, ginger, saffron, and turmeric are blended in different combinations to complement the taste of the food.

A typical meal in northern India consists of chapatis or rotis—breads made from dough that has been rolled flat and cooked on a griddle—stewed lentils or other legumes (called dal), vegetables, chutney (a sweet-sour condiment sauce), and pickles. In southern India, rice is the staple food and forms the basis of every meal. It is usually served with a thin vegetable soup, vegetables, and a dairy product such as yogurt. Rice pancakes are also popular. Many Indians finish their meal with an after-dinner *paan,* a betel leaf filled with spices and condiments. Tea, called chai, is the beverage of choice, usually served with milk and spices.

CHAI

Chai, or spiced tea, is sold premade in boxes, but it's fun to make this hot drink at home. This recipe can be made with regular or decaffeinated black tea.

- 4 c. water
- 1 3-inch cinnamon stick
- 1-inch piece fresh ginger root, cut into 4 slices
- ½ tsp. cardamom seeds
- ½ tsp. black peppercorns
- ½ tsp. whole cloves
- 1 tsp. whole coriander seeds
- 3 tea bags of black tea
- 1 cup milk
- honey or sugar to taste

1. Bring the water and spices to a boil in a saucepan. Reduce the heat, cover, and simmer for 20 minutes.
2. Add the tea bags and milk and simmer for an additional 3 or 4 minutes. Remove the tea bags, sweeten to taste, and serve, pouring the tea through a strainer to catch any floating spices.

For a stronger spice flavor, let the tea sit for a while and then reheat. Add more tea bags for a stronger black tea taste. Serves four.

Saris are the most popular form of women's clothing in India. Three weavers may work for ten days to create one silk sari.

Clothing

Because of India's generally hot climate, people wear light clothing in most areas of the country. Men typically wear Western-style shirts and trousers, especially in urban areas. In villages, men may wrap cloths around their bodies to form loose trousers, or they wear trousers that are loose around the waist and tightly fitted between the knee and ankle. The majority of Indian women wear a sari—a long piece of fabric draped like a dress, worn with a tightly fitted blouse underneath. Saris are brightly colored and may be made from cotton, silk, or another fabric. Another popular outfit among women is the *salwar kameez,* a long, loose tunic worn over pajama-like trousers.

Holidays and Festivals

The Indian calendar is one long procession of national, regional, local, religious, seasonal, and social festivals and holidays. Most holidays and festivals either follow the Indian lunar calendar, a complex system determined mainly by astrologers, or the Islamic calendar. The dates change, therefore, from year to year.

About fifteen public holidays are celebrated, although these vary from one place to another. Public holidays include some that are familiar to people in the West, such as New Year's Day, Easter, and Christmas. January 26 is Republic Day, celebrating the anniversary of India's establishment as a republic in 1950. A colorful military parade takes place on this day in Delhi. Independence Day is celebrated on August 15, and Mohandas Gandhi's birthday is observed on October 2.

Several public holidays are tied to religious festivals and observations. Important Muslim holidays include Id uz-Zuhu (Feast of the Sacrifice) in March; Muharram, the Islamic New Year, in March or April; and a festival marking the birth of Muhammad in June. The most important Muslim festival is Ramadan, which commemorates the Prophet's reception of the Quran (sacred text) from God.

During this holy month, which falls on at different times each year, Muslims fast from dawn to dusk. They close the end of Ramadan with a three-day feast called Eid al-Fitr.

Hindus celebrate scores of festivals associated with gods and goddesses and with nature. Major Hindu festivals include Diwali or Deepawali, Holi, Dussehra, Ganesh Chaturthi, Janmashthami, and Shiva Ratri. Diwali is a joyful festival of lights celebrated in October or November. During the five-day festivities, decorative oil lamps are lit at night to show the god Rama the way home from his period of exile. On this occasion, the house is given a thorough cleaning, decorative designs are painted on floors and walls, and families gather to offer prayers, exchange sweets, and light up their homes.

MEHNDI

For celebrations and ceremonies, including weddings, Hindu women decorate their hands with intricate designs of *mehndi*, or henna.

During the celebration of Holi, which marks the coming of spring, people light bonfires and good naturedly throw colored water and powder at each other. The popular Dussehra, also called Durga Puja, is dedicated to Rama's triumph over a demon king. This holiday, which takes place in September or October, is celebrated in different ways in different parts of India. In many places, the holiday culminates with the burning of huge images of the demon king Ravana. Bengali people spend ten days worshiping the goddess Durga, whose blessings Rama invoked before going into battle. Beautiful painted statues of the goddess are immersed in a river or pond on the ninth day of the festival.

Observers of **Dussehra** participate in the symbolic burning of the evil king Ravana.

THE ECONOMY

India has a strong and varied economic base. Wide-ranging economic reforms initiated during the early 1990s led to impressive growth into the beginning of the twenty-first century. Foreign investment in India and foreign trade increased tremendously, and India established itself as a leader in information technology. Yet it remains within the ranks of the world's poorest nations.

Until recently the Indian government controlled most major industries. In the early 1990s, the government loosened its grip on the economy and allowed producers to participate more freely in foreign markets. Heavy industry, banking, civil aviation, telecommunications, power generation, and large public building projects such as roads and ports were opened to private and foreign investment. In recent years, India has had one of the fastest growing economies in Asia.

Although industry has progressed, India's economy is still primarily based on services and agriculture. As a result, the economy is

vulnerable to drought and flood, and most farmers produce only enough crops to meet their families' needs.

Agriculture

Farming employs about 64 percent of India's working population, and agriculture provides roughly 27 percent of the nation's yearly income. Approximately half of India's land is under cultivation.

Most farms are small, family-tended plots. One sowing occurs after the monsoon rains begin in the floodplains, where rice, cotton, and jute thrive. Another planting season begins when the rains are over and involves crops like wheat, barley, and linseed. Commercial farming for export crops such as tea, coffee, and rubber often takes place on large plantations using hired labor.

Rice is the most important and the most widespread crop. India is the world's second largest producer and exporter of rice. Indian farmers cultivate many varieties of rice, generally in delta regions along the east coast. In 2000, workers harvested more than 87 million tons of rice.

Wheat, a staple in northern India, is the nation's second major food crop. Madhya Pradesh, Uttar Pradesh, and Punjab are among the main wheat-producing states. Other major crops include chickpeas, lentils and other legumes, potatoes, tobacco, spices, and peanuts and cashew nuts.

Tea is grown on large plantations in Assam, West Bengal, Kerala, and Tamil Nadu. Important during the colonial period, the tea harvest has continued to increase both in quantity and export value. Coffee is a smaller plantation crop, with about 250,000 tons (226,800 metric tons) produced in the late 1990s, mainly in Karnataka, Kerala, and Tamil Nadu.

India's vast textile industry is based on the nation's cotton crop, with about 12 million tons (10.9 million metric tons) produced. India is also a major cultivator of jute, a fibrous plant used to make burlap and twine. In the early 1990s, India emerged as a major sugarcane grower and produced nearly 300 million tons (272 million metric tons) by the end of the decade.

Workers at a Mumbai cotton mill operate an **industrial loom,** weaving Indian cotton into cloth. Ranked third largest international cotton producer, India provides about 13 percent of the world's cotton.

A traditional farmer tills his family field with an **ox-drawn plow.** About one-third of the cattle in the world are in India. Indians rarely butcher cattle.

India has a large livestock population, including more cattle and buffalo than any other country in the world. Because Hinduism regards cows as sacred and discourages the eating of beef, cattle are rarely slaughtered. Most Indians use cows for milking and as labor animals. Poultry and sheep are the main sources of meat, although few Indians can afford meat as part of their daily diet.

Services and Transportation

A growing urban population and increasing commercial and communication links between India and the rest of the world have contributed to an expansion in India's service industry, which includes government, tourism, and transportation. This sector contributes about 45 percent of India's gross domestic product (the total value of the goods and services produced in a year) and employs about one-fifth of the population.

Government is the largest service industry. India's tourism industry is growing, although it is subject to national and international events such as terrorist attacks. Other important services include computer programming, education, banking, health care, insurance, real estate, and transportation.

India has the one of the world's largest railway systems. The government-owned network has about 39,000 miles (63,000 km) of track and carries approximately 4.5 billion passengers each year. India's railways employ more than 1 million workers. About 5,000 miles (8,000 km) of navigable inland waterways supplement the railway system, and 2 million miles (3.2 million km) of roads crisscross the subcontinent.

Air India and Indian Airlines connect major cities within India and link the nation to more than twenty countries on five continents. Five main international airports and many smaller airfields operate throughout the country.

Industry and Mining

Industry, including mining, manufacturing, power, and construction, accounted for 26 percent of India's economy in 1998 and employed about 19 percent of the working population. The Indian government still owns and operates some important industries, including defense equipment, military aircraft and warships, nuclear energy, coal and lignite, and some chemicals and fertilizers. Among large industries, textile manufacturing employs the most people—about 64 million in the mid-1990s. Small handicraft businesses also employ millions of people.

The information technology industry, particularly software manufacturing, has become increasingly important, with about one thousand companies exporting software. The industry's center is Bangalore in the state of Karnataka. Other major software producers are based in Chennai, Hyderabad, Mumbai, and Pune.

India's Silicon Valley

Home to much of India's booming software industry, the city of Bangalore is referred to as the Silicon Valley of India. About 60 percent of software exports come from this southern city in the state of Karnataka.

The software industry actually started in Mumbai during the early 1980s, but the high cost of living and poor infrastructure drove information technology (IT) developers to set up business elsewhere—especially in Bangalore, where the Indian software giant Infosys is based. Multinational companies have established bases in the city, taking advantage of expert talent graduating from South India's colleges.

Much of India's **iron mining** takes place in the states of Bihar, Goa, Karnataka, Madhya Pradesh, and Orissa.

Other important manufacturing products include food products, iron and steel, industrial chemicals, diesel engines, electrical machinery, leather goods, motorcycles, passenger cars and other vehicles, and cement. India is also a large supplier of cut diamonds. Small-scale industries that contribute to India's economy produce works of brass, marble, ivory, wood, silk, and cotton.

The main raw materials for making steel—coal and iron ore—are abundant in India. In 1999 the country was the third largest coal producer in the world after China and the United States. Iron ore deposits lie mainly in Bihar, Madhya Pradesh, and Orissa. Mining complexes also extract limestone, bauxite (the raw material for aluminum), chromite, copper, manganese, gold, lead, zinc, and diamonds.

Although large natural gas and oil reserves lie within India and off its shores, the nation still imports large amounts of petroleum to meet its demand. Oil, natural gas, and coal provide about three-fourths of the nation's energy. India's industrial sector uses most of the country's coal to power its factories. Hydropower plants supply about one-fourth of the nation's power. But this supply is determined by seasonal water flow, which depends on monsoon rains. Further development of potential hydropower sites in the Himalayas is limited because of difficult access and a lack of urban centers in the region.

Nuclear-powered reactors have been built in Mumbai and Chennai and in the states of Rajasthan and Uttar Pradesh. But costs to construct such plants are high, and India currently gets only 2 percent of its electricity from nuclear power. In some rural areas, electricity is scarce, and residents rely on wood for fuel.

Forestry and Fishing

Much of India's previously forested areas now support only scrub vegetation, and deforestation has reduced the percentage of wooded land to about one-fifth of the nation's total territory. Commercial forestry takes place in the Western Ghats, western Himalayas, and hilly areas in central India but is not a large part of the country's economy.

Fishing is a growing industry in India, taking place along the coastlines and in the many inland rivers and waterways. The major fishing states are Kerala, Tamil Nadu, and Maharashtra in the south. Of freshwater fish, catfish and carp are most important. Saltwater catches include mackerel, croakers, drums, Bombay duck, sardines, herring, anchovies, tuna, and shrimp.

Fishers market most of their hauls as fresh fish. The remainder are dried, frozen, or otherwise prepared for storage and shipment. Exports of fish products have increased significantly in the last decade.

The Indian **forestry industry** harvests trees from large tree plantations. More than half of India's forests are plantations.

A cargo ship laden with Indian exports prepares to set out to sea. India exports more than $30 billion in goods each year. Germany, Japan, the United Kingdom, and the United States are India's main trading partners.

Foreign Trade

India's trade links with the rest of the world have increased since the economic reforms of the early 1990s, and global trade has played a crucial role in the country's economic development. While the number of goods and services that India exports has grown, the country still imports more than it exports.

India's major imports include petroleum and petroleum products, fertilizers, pearls and gemstones, and electronic goods, as well as equipment and raw materials for industrial production, such as iron, steel, heavy machinery, and chemicals and metals.

India exports some 7,500 products to about two hundred countries. The most important exports are gems and jewelry, clothing, engineering products, cotton yarn and fabrics, chemicals, and leather goods. Many agricultural products, such as tea, coffee, fish, rice, and spices, contribute to India's export trade. Computer software exports have increased significantly, earning about $4 billion in 2000. The main export markets are the United States, Japan, the United Kingdom, and Germany.

Women at Work

The Self-Employed Women's Association (SEWA) is a labor union for self-employed women in India. The union was founded in 1972 in Ahmadabad, Gujarat, by a group of poor women who pooled their meager earnings to form their own cooperative bank. SEWA branches exist all over India.

The bank remains an important part of the organization, extending credit to members and offering women—many of whom cannot read or write—the opportunity to improve their economic situation.

You can find a link to SEWA's website at vgs.com.

CHILD LABOR

Many children in India do not spend the day in school but at work—in factories, in the fields, or on the street. India has the largest child labor force in the world, with as many as 80 million children working. The poorest families in India often regard a child as another set of hands to contribute to the family income. Some parents allow their children to work as bonded laborers (the child works at a factory in exchange for a small loan to the parents). But, in many cases, the loan cannot be repaid.

India's government and many domestic and international groups strive to find ways to reduce child labor. A program called Rugmark, for example, labels carpets to show that they have been made without child labor. Despite these efforts, many Indian children are still working, deprived of an education.

The Future

India passed two important milestones in recent years. In 1997 Indians celebrated fifty years of independence. And in 2000, the country surpassed the one-billion mark in population. India has made steady progress in reducing poverty and illiteracy and in strengthening the economy. Despite the rise of Hindu nationalism as a dominant political force, India's democracy is working, with a free press and a judicial system that provides a check on the executive and legislative branches of government. The country is rich in cultural diversity and human and natural resources.

India's greatest challenge is to control population growth, which is straining the environment and natural resources. This, in turn, is making agriculture more expensive and less sustainable. India's cities and rivers are polluted, leading to health problems. The increasing population makes it more difficult to combat poverty and illiteracy.

The divide is increasing between India's growing middle class, who are educated, live in modern cities, have good jobs, and enjoy a decent

Looking to the future, India is investing in **education.** A rapidly growing population and poverty are major challenges to the effort.

standard of living, and the millions of poor people in the countryside and the city slums. They struggle to earn a living, face malnutrition and disease with inadequate access to health care, and may not be educated.

Another major challenge for India is the ongoing conflict with Pakistan over the state of Jammu and Kashmir. The fact that both countries have a nuclear arsenal makes the need to resolve the conflict even more urgent. India has much at stake in trying to keep the peace, not only with Pakistan, but also among Muslims and Hindus and other ethnic and religious groups within its borders.

We are
birds of the
same nest,
We may wear different skins,
We may speak different languages
We may believe in different religions,
We may belong to different cultures,
Yet we share the same home. . . .

We must learn to
happily progress together
Or miserably perish together,
For man can live individually
But survive only together.

—from the Atharva Veda,
one of the Hindu scriptures

c. 4000 B.C.	Humans establish communal villages in what is now India.
c. 2500–1800 B.C.	Indus Valley civilization flourishes along Indus River, with urban centers at Mohenjo-Daro and Harappa.
c. 2000–1000 B.C.	Aryans arrive in India from south-central Asia.
c. 1500–1200 B.C.	Aryans compose the Vedas, which form the basis of Hindu religion.
c. 500 B.C.	Buddhism is founded by Siddhartha Gautama (Buddha). Jainism is founded by Vardhamana Mahavira.
321 B.C.	Magadha ruler Chandragupta Maurya comes to power, beginning the Maurya dynasty.
272–232 B.C.	Ashoka reigns over Mauryan Empire.
230 B.C.–A.D. 230	Andhra dynasty rules in southern India.
A.D. 300–500	Gupta dynasty rules during the "golden age of India."
499	Mathematician and astronomer Aryabhatta writes scientific treatise, *Aryabhatiya*.
632	The prophet Muhammad, founder of Islam, dies. Muslims begin arriving in India.
c. 900–1000	Chola dynasty expands empire in southern India.
1206–1526	Muslim rulers, the Delhi sultanate, control northern India.
1336	Vijayanagar kingdom is founded in southern India.
1498	Portuguese navigator Vasco da Gama reaches India.
c. 1500–1700	Indian miniature painting flourishes.
1526–30	Babur founds Mughal Empire.
1600s	British East India Company establishes several trading posts in India.
1632	Emperor Shah Jahan begins construction of the Taj Mahal.
1757	Britain gains control of Bengal after the Battle of Plassey.
1857	Indians rebel against British control of India in Sepoy Mutiny, or First War of Independence. The British victory leads to establishment of British colonial government.
1885	Indian professionals form Indian National Congress to promote self-rule.

1906 The All-India Muslim League (later called the Muslim League) is organized.

1913 Poet Rabindranath Tagore wins the Nobel Prize for Literature.

1919 Demonstrations against British become widespread. British troops fire on unarmed demonstrators in Amritsar in the Amritsar Massacre.

1920 Mohandas K. Gandhi becomes leader of the Indian National Congress and begins program of nonviolent civil disobedience against the British.

1947 British Empire transfers power to new, independent nations of India and Pakistan. Jawaharlal Nehru becomes first prime minister of independent India.

1948 Mohandas K. Gandhi is assassinated.

1950 Constitution of India is adopted.

1965 India and Pakistan go to war over disputed territory in Kashmir.

1966 Indira Gandhi becomes prime minister. The Soviet Union brokers a peace accord between India and Pakistan.

1975 Indira Gandhi declares a state of emergency, jailing opponents and suspending the Constitution.

1979 Mother Teresa wins the Nobel Peace Prize.

1984 Indira Gandhi sends troops to dislodge Sikh militants from occupation of Golden Temple in Amritsar. Sikhs are killed there and in Delhi. Gandhi is assassinated by Sikh bodyguards in October; her son Rajiv becomes prime minister.

1991 Rajiv Gandhi is assassinated.

1992 Hindus construct Hindu temple on site of ancient Islamic mosque. Hindu-Muslim violence breaks out across country.

1996 Congress Party is voted out of office, but elections are inconclusive, leaving no overall majority in Parliament. Hindu Bharatiya Janata Party, among others, attempts to form new government.

1997 India celebrates fifty years of independence. Novelist Arundhati Roy wins Booker Prize for *The God of Small Things.*

1998 India conducts underground nuclear explosions. Pakistan responds by carrying out its own nuclear tests.

2001 A devastating earthquake hits the state of Gujurat. India cooperates with United States in war against terrorists and Taliban rulers in Afghanistan.

2002 India and Pakistan threaten to engage in a new war over Kashmir, and both countries mobilize their militaries along the so-called Line of Control, or border.

COUNTRY NAME Republic of India (the Sanskrit name for India is Bharat)

AREA 1,269,340 square miles (3,287,590 sq. km)

MAIN LANDFORMS Himalaya Mountains, Indo-Gangetic Plain, Deccan Plateau

HIGHEST POINT Mount Kanchenjunga (28,146 feet/8,598 m above sea level)

LOWEST POINT Sea level

MAJOR RIVERS Ganges, Indus, Brahmaputra, Narmada, Mahanadi, Godavari, Krishna, Cauvery

ANIMALS Tigers, elephants, monkeys, camels, antelopes, wild boar, crocodiles, peacocks, Indian cobras

CAPITAL CITY New Delhi

OTHER MAJOR CITIES Mumbai (Bombay), Kolkata (Calcutta), Hyderabad, Chennai (Madras), Bangalore

OFFICIAL LANGUAGES Hindi is the principal official language, but the Constitution recognizes eighteen official languages, including English, Sanskrit, Bengali, Punjabi, Urdu, Marathi, and Gujarati.

MONETARY UNIT Rupee. 100 paisa = 1 rupee.

INDIAN CURRENCY

India's monetary unit is the rupee. *Rupee* comes from the Sanskrit word *rupya,* meaning "wrought silver." The rupee has been used since about the fourth or fifth century B.C.

The rupee is divided into 100 paisa. Coins come in denominations of 5, 10, 20, 25, and 50 paisa, as well as 1, 2, and 5 rupees. Paper currency is printed in denominations of 10, 20, 50, 100, and 500 rupees. On paper currency notes of 5 rupees or larger, fourteen different languages are represented. Indian coins contain the national emblem, the Lion of Sarnath, a stone pillar erected to mark the spot where Buddha preached his first sermon after being enlightened.

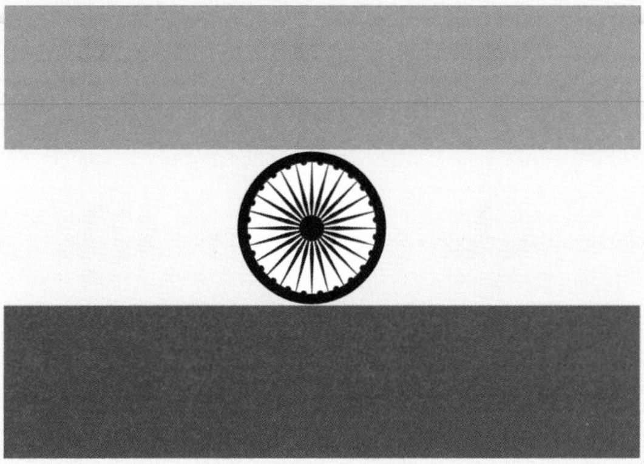

The Indian flag was adopted in 1947, the year India gained independence from Great Britain. India's first prime minister, Jawaharlal Nehru, called the flag a symbol of freedom not just for Indians, but for all people.

The flag has three horizontal stripes: saffron (orange) across the top, white in the center, and dark green at the bottom. The saffron stands for courage and sacrifice; the white for purity and truth; the green for faith and fertility. In the center of the white stripe is a dark blue wheel, an ancient symbol called the Dharma Chakra, or wheel of law. The wheel symbolizes the cycles of life and fate.

The wheel also is sometimes viewed as a spinning wheel. This image was derived from Mohandas Gandhi's call for economic self-sufficiency through hand-spinning.

"Jana Gana Mana" ("Morning Song of India") was composed by the famous poet Rabindranath Tagore and was first sung at a session of the Indian National Congress in Kolkata in December 1911. The song was adopted as India's national anthem on January 24, 1950, two days before the Constitution came into effect. With patriotism and exhortations of victory, the song refers to many different regions of the country. Tagore himself translated the hymn into English. Here is the first stanza:

Jana Gana Mana

Thou art the ruler of the minds of all people,
dispenser of India's destiny.
Thy name rouses the hearts of Punjab, Sind, Gujarat and Maratha,
Of the Dravida and Orissa and Bengal;
It echoes in the hills of the Vindhyas and Himalayas,
mingles in the music of Yamuna and Ganga
and is chanted by the waves of the Indian Sea.
They pray for thy blessings and sing thy praise.
The saving of all people waits in thy hand,
thou dispenser of India's destiny,
Victory, victory, victory to thee.

For a link to a site where you can listen to India's national anthem, "Jana Gana Mana," go to vgsbooks.com.

B. R. AMBEDKAR (1891–1956) Born into an untouchable family in western India, Ambedkar excelled at school and was awarded a scholarship to study law. After earning his degree, he practiced law and established a reputation as leader of the "depressed classes." He envisioned a casteless India and struggled for the rights of untouchables, or Dalits. In 1947 Ambedkar helped frame the Constitution, which outlawed discrimination based on caste.

ARYABHATTA (A.D. 476–550) This great mathematician and astronomer was born in Kerala and studied at the University of Nalanda. In 499 he wrote the Aryabhatiya, a summary of calculations in mathematics and astronomy written in verse. Among his greatest contributions were the discovery of zero and decimals, the introduction of trigonometry, and an approximation of the value of pi (the ratio of the circumference of a circle to its diameter).

BUDDHA (C. 563–483 B.C.) The founder of the Buddhist religion began life as an Indian prince, Siddhartha Gautama. He left his comfortable home in the foothills of the Himalayas at the age of twenty-nine and, after a six-year spiritual quest, he attained enlightenment while meditating under a tree at Bodhgaya.

INDIRA GANDHI (1917–1984) The only child of Jawaharlal Nehru, she was born in Allahabad and educated in India and England. She married fellow Congress Party member Feroze Gandhi (no relation to Mohandas) and served as prime minister from 1966 to 1977 and from 1980 to 1984. In June 1984, she ordered an attack on the Sikh holy shrine, the Golden Temple of Amritsar. Five months later, she was killed by two of her Sikh bodyguards.

MOHANDAS K. (MAHATMA) GANDHI (1869–1948) One of India's most beloved heroes, Gandhi was born in Gujarat and trained as a lawyer in London. He developed the technique of nonviolent agitation called *satyagraha,* which means "devotion to truth" or "moral domination." Gandhi became the leader of the Congress Party and launched a series of mass civil disobedience movements against the British Raj, including the Quit India movement in 1942. Gandhi, who was given the title of Mahatma, or "Great Soul," was assassinated in 1948 by a Hindu fanatic.

MOTHER TERESA (1910–1997) Known for her lifetime of service to poor people in the slums of Kolkata and other cities in India, Mother Teresa was born in Skopje, Macedonia, as Agnes Gonxha Bojaxhia. At the age of eighteen, she joined a group of Roman Catholic nuns who were active in India. In 1947 she received a call, or message from God, to leave the convent and help the poorest of the poor. Mother Teresa received the Nobel Peace Prize in 1979.

MIRA NAIR (b. 1957) Born in Bhubaneshwar in the state of Orissa, accomplished film director, writer, and producer Mira Nair was educated at Delhi and Harvard Universities. She began her career as an actor, then started making documentary films on the streets of Delhi. Her first feature film, *Salaam Bombay!,* won 25 international awards and was nominated for an Academy Award. Her 2001 film *Monsoon Wedding* was the highest-grossing Indian film released in the United States.

JAWAHARLAL NEHRU (1889–1964) Born of a family of wealthy Brahmans from Kashmir, Jawaharlal Nehru was educated in England. Along with Gandhi, Nehru was a leader in the Indian nationalist movement. Nehru became the first prime minister of the new, independent republic, serving from 1947 until his death in 1964.

SATYAJIT RAY (1921–1992) Born and raised in Kolkata, Ray is considered one of the greatest filmmakers of the twentieth century. He brought international recognition to Indian cinema with his 1955 motion picture *Pather Panchali (The Song of the Road)* and its two sequels, known as the Apu trilogy.

ARUNDHATI ROY (b. 1961) Born in Bengal, Roy grew up in the southern state of Kerala and trained as an architect in Delhi. She wrote film scripts before publishing her novel *The God of Small Things,* which won the prestigious Booker Prize in 1997. A committed social activist, Roy has immersed herself in causes such as the antinuclear movement.

SALMAN RUSHDIE (b. 1947) The son of a Muslim businessman of Mumbai, Rushdie was educated in England and makes his home in London. His second novel, *Midnight's Children,* won England's prestigious Booker Prize in 1981. His 1989 novel *The Satanic Verses* was denounced by Muslim spiritual leaders.

RAVI SHANKAR (b. 1920) As the foremost sitar player in the world, Shankar was influential in stimulating Western appreciation of Indian music. Born in Benares (later Varanasi), Shankar studied music and dance. During his long career, Shankar founded the National Orchestra of India, composed film music, and performed thousands of concerts worldwide. Shankar's daughter Anoushka is following in his footsteps, and the two tour together.

RABINDRANATH TAGORE (1861–1941) A towering figure in Indian culture, Tagore was a multifaceted genius—a poet, song composer, playwright, short story writer, essayist, and painter. The son of a Bengali religious reformer, Tagore wrote verses from an early age and began publishing books of poetry when he was in his twenties. He was awarded the Nobel Prize for Literature in 1913 for his collection of poems, *Gitanjali.*

Cave Temples Dating back more than two thousand years, these temples in Ajanta and Ellora are not actual caves but sculpture and architecture chiseled from the solid rock of the area's hills.

Chowpatty Beach This Mumbai beach is alive with food stalls, carnival rides, and vendors and is a favorite place for an evening stroll.

Corbett Tiger Reserve This tiger reserve adjoins a wildlife sanctuary in the foothills of the Himalayas. Visitors may see elephants, macaques and other monkeys, peacocks, several types of deer, crocodiles, wild boars—and, if they're lucky, a tiger.

Golden Temple The holiest shrine of the Sikh religion, this marble temple in Amritsar is a blend of Hindu and Muslim styles. It has a golden dome and is surrounded by a sacred pool.

Hampi This ancient city (also known as Vijayanagar) was the capital of the largest Hindu empire in South India before the 1500s. The ruins are a jumble of vast stone temples, elephant stables, and palaces.

Jaipur The capital of the state of Rajasthan is known as the pink city for the color of the buildings in the old walled quarter. The city is full of palaces and temples in an assortment of architectural styles.

Jama Masjid The largest mosque in India, this monument faces the Red Fort in Old Delhi.

Maidan The "green lung" of Kolkata was cleared around Fort William, established by the British in 1757 and still standing. Within the grounds of the large park are gardens, a racecourse, cricket and soccer fields, and the Victoria Memorial.

Red Fort Mughal emperor Shah Jahan began construction of the massive Red Fort in Delhi in 1638. The monument's huge red sandstone walls extend for nearly a mile (1.6 km).

Shore Temple The stone temple at Mallapuram (also known as Mahabalipuram) was built in the seventh century A.D. by Dravidian people.

Taj Mahal Known as the eighth wonder of the world, this white marble monument in Agra was begun in 1632 by the Mughal ruler Shah Jahan as a memorial to his favorite wife, Mumtaz Mahal, who died in childbirth.

Varanasi (Benares) The rising sun casts a golden glow on this holy city on the Ganges River. Thousands of devout Hindus bathe in the river here each day to purify their souls.

Adivasis: tribal people in India. Since ancient times, the Adivasis lived in the hills and forests, particularly in the northeastern part of the country, but increasing pressure for land forced many tribal people off their ancestral lands and into poverty.

Aryan: Sanskrit word for "noble"; people who migrated from south-central Asia to northern India around 1500 B.C.

Brahman: a member of the priest caste, the highest Hindu caste

caste: an ancient system of hereditary social classes in Hinduism that determines a person's place in society. The caste system was outlawed by the Constitution in 1950 but still wields influence.

Dalit: a member of the untouchable class

dharma: a Hindu concept referring to an individual's duty or moral code of behavior

Dravidians: people who are descended from some of India's earliest inhabitants. Dravidians migrated to southern India after the arrival of the Aryans in about 1500 B.C.

karma: a concept in Hinduism and Buddhism that holds that one's destiny is determined by actions in past lives

monsoon: seasonal winds that bring heavy rains. India has two monsoon seasons, the southwest monsoon beginning in late May or early June, and the northeast or retreating monsoon in October and November.

mosque: a Muslim place of worship

nationalism: loyalty or devotion to a nation, characterized by promoting the interests and culture of one nation or group above all others

panchayat: village council. Members of village councils serve five-year terms and act as intermediaries between villages and state or territorial governments.

Partition: the 1947 division of India into two countries, India and Pakistan. Partition led to bloodshed and violence as Muslims in India fled to Pakistan and Hindus and Sikhs in Pakistan fled to India.

sari: a woman's garment consisting of a long piece of fabric draped like a dress, worn with a tightly fitted blouse underneath. Saris are typically made of silk or cotton.

satyagraha: "devotion to truth" or "moral domination"; a philosophy of nonviolent protest developed and practiced by Mohandas K. Gandhi as a form of resistance to British colonial rule.

Vedas: Hindu sacred books of verse, written by the Aryans, which form the foundation of Hinduism. The Vedas tell epic stories about how the Aryans lived and how the gods created the universe.

Crossette, Barbara. *India: Old Civilization in a New World.* New York: Foreign Policy Association, 2000.
This overview of India, written by a *New York Times* journalist, covers historical and recent events and looks at India's current challenges.

***The Europa World Yearbook, 2001.* London: Europa Publications Limited, 2002.**
This annual publication includes statistics on everything from agriculture and tourism to education and population density, as well as the latest details about India's educational system, administration, defense, energy, and natural resources. Key statistics and historical events are given for each state.

***India.* Footscray, Australia: Lonely Planet Publications, 2001.**
Lonely Planet's travel guide to India provides a wealth of information on history, society, culture, and people. The book includes recent information on new states, name changes, and political events.

Johnson, Gordon. *Cultural Atlas of India: India, Pakistan, Nepal, Bhutan, Bangladesh and Sri Lanka.* New York: Facts on File, 1996.
This amply illustrated guide presents an overview of the culture and history of India, with a description of the neighboring countries in the region.

Library of Congress, Federal Research Division. *India—A Country Study,* 2002.
Website: <http://lcweb2.loc.gov/frd/cs/intoc.html> **(July 26, 2002).**
The Library of Congress gives an overview of India's history, geography, demographics, religious life, languages, social structure, economy, government, and other aspects of society.

Mistry, Rohinton. *A Fine Balance.* New York: Alfred A. Knopf, 1996.
In this sweeping tragedy, four social outcasts struggle to survive during India's State of Emergency in 1975.

Population Reference Bureau. *Population Reference Bureau,* 2002.
Website: <http://www.prb.org/> **(July 27, 2002).**
The annual statistics on this site provide data on India's population, birth and death rates, fertility rate, infant mortality rate, and other useful demographic information.

Silvers, Robert B., and Barbara Epstein, eds. *India: A Mosaic.* New York: New York Review of Books, 2000.
With an introduction by novelist Arundhati Roy, this collection of essays looks at many aspects of contemporary India and includes a CD of Indian music.

Sridhar, S. N., and Nirmal K. Mattoo, eds. *Ananya: A Portrait of India.* New York: The Association of Indians in America, 1997.
This wide-ranging collection of essays by scholars and experts on India includes chapters on history, religion and philosophy, society and politics, science and technology, business and economics, art and architecture, language and literature, performing arts, people, and leaders.

Statistical Abstract of the World.
Detroit: Gale Research, 1997.
This is the source to turn to for economic and social data worldwide. You'll also find a comprehensive directory of each country's government, diplomatic representation, press, and trade organizations.

Turner, Barry, ed. *The Statesman's Yearbook: The Politics, Cultures, and Economics of the World, 2001.* New York: Macmillan Press, 2000.
This reference presents statistical information on population, trade, and economy. It also contains a detailed account of India's history and current events, government, military, economy, social welfare, and education.

United Nations, Department of Statistical Affairs. *United Nations Statistics Division,* 2002.
Website: <http://www.un.org/Depts/unsd/> (July 27, 2002).
This UN website provides a wide range of statistical information, including economic, environmental, social, and demographic data.

Van Der Veer, Peter. *Religious Nationalism: Hindus and Muslims in India.* Berkeley: University of California Press, 1994.
This book examines the relationship between religion and politics in India, focusing on the bloody 1992 confrontation over the Babri mosque in Ayodhya.

Census of India
Website: <**http://www.censusindia.net**>
The Indian government's national census website contains statistics and maps showing various measures of population.

Dommermuth-Costa, Carol. ***Indira Gandhi: Daughter of India.*** **Minneapolis: Lerner Publications Company, 2001.**
This biography traces the life of the only woman who has served as prime minister of India.

Forster, E. M. ***A Passage to India.*** **San Diego: Harcourt Brace Jovanovich, 1984.**
This classic novel, first published in 1924, revolves around the friendship between an Englishman and an Indian man during the British colonial era.

Government of India Ministry of External Affairs
Website: <**http://www.meadev.nic.in**>
This government website is an excellent source of information on many aspects of life in India, including current news, culture, economy, media, sports, and tourism.

Hindunet—The Hindu Universe
Website: <**http://www.hindunet.org**>
This website devoted to Hindu religion and culture includes a glossary of Hindu terms and information about temples, festivals, beliefs, and other aspects of Hinduism.

India.org
Website: <**http://www.india.org**>
This portal site gives links to general information about India, with an emphasis on popular culture.

Indian Recipes
Website: <**http://www.indianrecipes.com**>
This website offers a searchable database of Indian cooking, recipes, foods, and a glossary.

Itihaas: The History of India
Website: <**http://www.itihaas.com**>
This site is a good resource for Indian history.

Madavan, Vijay. ***Cooking the Indian Way.*** **Minneapolis: Lerner Publications Company, 2002.**
This cookbook discusses Indian food, culture, and holidays and serves up many delectable recipes, including recipes for holiday and vegetarian fare.

Maps of India
Website: <**http://www.mapsofindia.com**>
Among the many different maps found on this website are political, geographical, topographical, and historical maps, as well as maps featuring cities, states, and languages.

Martin, Christopher. ***Mohandas Gandhi.*** **Minneapolis: Lerner Publications Company, 2001.**
This biography tells the story of India's greatest spiritual and political leader.

Mehta, Gita. *Snakes and Ladders: Glimpses of Modern India.* New York: Nan A. Talese/Doubleday, 1997.
The author of several books and articles about India, including the novel *A River Sutra,* offers an entertaining collection of essays on a wide range of topics from politics to trees to Indian decor.

Naipaul, V. S. *An Area of Darkness.* New York: Macmillan, 1965.
Naipaul, born in Trinidad of Indian descent, describes his first visit to the homeland he had never seen. Naipaul won the Nobel Prize for Literature in 2001.

Nehru, Jawaharlal. *The Discovery of India.* New York: John Day, 1946.
The founder of modern India provides a view of Indian history.

Roy, Arundhati. *The God of Small Things.* New York: Random House, 1997.
Winner of England's Booker Prize in 1997, this novel encompasses love, betrayal, and tragedy against the backdrop of the social and political landscape of the southern Indian state of Kerala.

Rushdie, Salman. *Midnight's Children.* New York: Penguin, 1995.
Rushdie's 1980 masterpiece tells the tale of children born on the eve of India's independence in 1947 and shows how their lives evolve along with the nation.

Silvers, Robert B., and Barbara Epstein. *India: A Mosaic.* New York: New York Review of Books, 2000.
With an introduction by Arundhati Roy, this collection of essays offers insights into the history, politics, and culture of India and includes a CD of Indian music.

The Times of India
Website: <**http://www.timesofindia.com**>
The website of of one of the most widely read and influential daily newspapers in India is a good source of current news about India and the world.

vgsbooks.com
Website: <**http://www.vgsbooks.com**>
Visit vgsbooks.com, the homepage of the Visual Geography Series®. You can get linked to all sorts of useful online information, including geographical, historical, demographic, cultural, and economic websites. The vgsbooks.com site is a great resource for late-breaking news and statistics.

Welcome to India
Website: <**http://www.tourindia.com**>
This site offers a range of articles about travel and tourism in India.

Captions for photos appearing on cover and chapter openers:

Cover: The architecture of this Sikh temple in New Delhi reflects Islamic influences in the Sikh religion and culture. Guru Nanak founded Sikhism in the late 1400s, combining elements of the Islamic and Hindu faiths.

pp. 4–5 Celebrants of the festival of Holi dress in colorful clothing and playfully throw colored water and powders at one another in anticipation of spring. Originally a Hindu festival, Holi has become a national holiday celebrated in the month of March.

pp. 8–9 The Greater Himalaya Mountains rise up in Jammu and Kashmir.

pp. 20–21 The haunting remains of Mohenjo-Daro stand in testament to India's earliest civilization. The ancient city, located in what is now Pakistan, flourished between 2500–1800 B.C. in the Indus River Valley.

pp. 38–39 Pedestrians filling a street in Mumbai stop for the camera before going on with their busy day.

pp. 46–47 The Shore Temple at Mallapuram (also known as Mahabalipuram) in the state of Tamil Nadu. The temple was built in the seventh century A.D. by the Pallavas, a Dravidian people, and is dedicated to the Hindu gods Shiva and Vishnu.

pp. 56–57 An Indian farmer tends to a new crop of rice.

Photo Acknowledgments
The images in this book are used with the permission of: © Lindsay Hebberd/CORBIS, pp. 4–5, 55 (bottom); Ron Bell/PresentationMaps.com, pp. 6, 10; © Wolfgang Kaehler, pp. 7, 8–9, 11, 14 (left and right), 16 (top), 44, 46–47, 50, 54; Michele Burgess, pp. 12, 41, 52 (top), 59; Nevada Wier, pp. 13, 40 (right); © R. A. Acharya/Dinodia, p. 15; © Dinodia, 23, 33 (left), 38–39, 43, 48, 52 (bottom), 58, 64–65; © Betty Crowell, pp. 16–17 (bottom), 26, 40 (left), 42; © Ruthie Soudack, p. 19; Embassy of Pakistan, pp. 20–21; North Wind Picture Archives, p. 22; © Robert Holmes/CORBIS, p. 24; © SEF/Art Resource, NY, p. 25; © Maxine Cass, p. 28, 51; © Hulton|Archive/Getty Images, pp. 30 (top), 30–31 (bottom); Independent Picture Service, p. 33 (right); © Reuters NewMedia Inc./CORBIS, p. 35 (top), 36, 60; © AFP/CORBIS, p. 35 (bottom), 37; © T. S. Satyan/Dinodia, p. 45; Amrit P. Singh/wildphotos.com, p. 55 (top); Anil Dev/wildphotos.com, pp. 56–57; © TRIP/Dinodia, p. 61, 63; © TRIP/Jody Denham, p. 62; © Todd Strand/Independent Picture Service, p. 68.

Cover photo: © Wolfgang Kaehler

Back Cover photo: NASA